THE 100+ SERIES™

Reproducible Activities

After School Writing Activities

Grade 4

S0-ADO-182

Published by Instructional Fair • TS Denison
an imprint of

McGraw Hill **Children's Publishing**

Editors: Susan Fitzgerald, Bruce Walker, Alyson Kieda

 Children's Publishing

Published by Instructional Fair • TS Denison
An imprint of McGraw-Hill Children's Publishing
Copyright © 2003 McGraw-Hill Children's Publishing

Send all inquiries to:
McGraw-Hill Children's Publishing
3195 Wilson Drive NW
Grand Rapids, Michigan 49544

After School Writing Activities—grade 4
ISBN: 0-7424-1784-0

1 2 3 4 5 6 7 8 9 PHXBK 08 07 06 05 04 03
The McGraw·Hill Companies

Table of Contents

Writer's Toolbox
Look! 5
Listen! 6
Touch! 7
Ah, the Aroma! 8
Stars Danced in the Sky 9
Like Distant Drums 10
My Brother Was a Prince 11
Clearly Confused 12
Strong as an Ox! 13
Ribbit 14
Blast! Roar! Crossword 15
Comes and Goes Crossword 16
Thesaurus 17
Chuckled 18
Widely Grinned 19
Animal Expressions 20
The New World 21
The Tipsy Tugboat Tooted Its Horn 22
All the King's Horses 23
"Oh, My!" 24
Writer's Toolbox Crossword 25

Story Elements
The New Kid 26
Bigfoot 27
First... Next... Then... 28
Walfredo and the Cat 29
Developing Characters 30
Describing Characters 31
A Day in Your Life 32
Setting the Scene 33
Grabs Your Interest 34
Tornado Warning! 35
And She Lived Happily Ever After 36
The Title Is Vital 37
Hoot! 38
Mrs. O'Leary's Cow 39
Wrapping It Up 40
Welcome to the Show! 41
Mystery at the Museum 42
Missing Ring 43
Solving the Case 44
Showing How You Feel 45
Putting It All Together 46

True Stories
My Stories 47
Writing a Biography 48
Writing an Autobiography 49
And So, My Fellow Americans... 50–51
Why I Should Keep Morgan 52
Volcano Erupts! 53
A Good Book 54
You're the Movie Critic 55
The Reporter's "Five and One" Rule 56
Breaking News! 57
Farmer Spots UFO 58
Writing Ads for Products 59
My Favorite Holiday 60
Thinking of You 61

Today I... 62
Writing a Letter to a Friend 63
Writing a Business Letter 64
Sunset 65
What Does the Future Hold? 66
Digging Up Ancient History 67
All That Jazz 68
I Wish Upon a Star 69
Four Seasons 70
My Favorite Vacation Spot 71
How Do You Do? 72
Living Longer 73
Water, Water Everywhere 74

Imagination
Realistic Fiction 75
Science Fiction 76–77
All the World's a Stage 78–79
Seeing with Your Ears 80
What's That Sound? 81
Red Badge of Courage 82–83
Armchair Critic 84
Lights, Camera, Action! 85
Writer in Wonderland 86
Knock, Knock 87
Punch Line 88–89
Can You Believe This? 90
Making Fun for Fun 91
Myths 92
Legends 93
The Moral of the Story 94
Detective Hilary 95
Monsters in the Basement 96
Somewhere in the Old West 97
Rock 'n' Roll Road Show 98
Once Upon a Time 99
Lost in the Wilderness 100
Story Launch 101–107

Poetry
Working Out with Words 108–109
Poetic Senses 110
Images and Emotions 111
I Wandered Lonely as a Cloud 112
Of Cabbages and Kings 113
Five-Line Fun 114
Japanese Poetic Forms 115–116
As White as the Snow 117
You Are a Glittering Star 118
Poetry Overview 119
What Do Songs Mean? 120

Proofreading
Please Elaborate 121
Using Commas Correctly 122
Writing Quotations Correctly 123
Making Subjects and Verbs Agree 124
Do You Hafe a Brother? 125
Proofreading Fun 126

Answer Key 127–128

Introduction

The activities in this book are designed for students to enjoy as after school activities to enhance their writing techniques and skills. These exercises will help students appreciate the beauty and sound of words, feel and hear the rhythms found in sentences, and learn the poetry and subtleties of language. Although these exercises are in simple-to-follow formats, each was created to be fun while communicating a fundamental writing skill.

In these activities, students will read, research, tell stories, design, dramatize, select, evaluate, collect, and share. They will perform narrative, descriptive, expository, and persuasive writing for both fiction and nonfiction. They will have many opportunities to experiment with language, using a variety of writing forms such as journals, book reports, fables, poetry, personal narratives, newspaper stories, puzzles, plays, cloze activities, and story starters.

A cloze activity is a fun writing tool, which encourages creativity and story building skills for the young writer. Students choose their own verbs, adjectives, adverbs, and nouns to fill in the line and complete each story. This is a wonderful way for them to use their imagination as well as practice their grammar skills.

A story starter is also a fun writing tool that starts students on their way to creating their own story by giving them the first sentence of a story. The activities in this book may be shared with a friend or worked on independently. They may also be used as pages for homework. Some exercises can be completed in one writing period but others may take longer.

Each student should have a notebook to use as a journal, folders or three-ring binders for completed writing projects, and a separate book for poetry. Students will enjoy reading through their compositions. With a separate book of poetry, they can also illustrate their poems.

Look!

A good writer uses words to paint a picture for the reader. Interesting writing allows the reader to **see** something in his or her mind. When writing, *don't tell* the reader what he or she should see—*show* the reader. A writer must watch his or her subject very carefully in order to describe its physical appearance, its actions, and its intentions.

For example, if you are writing a story about young horses playing in a field together, you will need to watch the horses at play. Watching them helps you notice the details that make the reader feel like he or she is there.

Jot down words and phrases that seem to describe best what you see. Your notes might include the following.

Describing the actions:
frisky frolicking   playful chasing   graceful prancing   rearing happily

Describing the horses:
- Chestnut with four white socks, white star, large soft brown eyes, stand-up mane, wispy tail, colt, long spindly legs
- Jet black, kind shining eyes, wild long mane, filly, smaller than the colt

Describing where the horses are playing:
emerald green, grassy field   shoulder-high white fence   trees with leaves like lace

Use these notes to paint a picture for the reader. As an option, observe, take notes, and write about something you see out your window.

Go to one of your favorite places with a friend. Sit and observe everything you see. Write lists that *show, not tell* why you like this place. Use plenty of details. Then combine your descriptions into paragraphs so your reader will see why this place is so special to you.

Name _____ Date _____

Listen!

Describing sounds in writing greatly adds to the reader's sense of what is going on. Here is an example of how the writer can help the reader to **hear**.

> Off in the distance, I heard a faint wail. It built into a crescendo and became a shrill cry. As it neared the intersection, the loud horn screamed and I jumped back farther away from the curb. The fire truck sped down the street and the ear-piercing sound of the siren gradually faded away.

Choose one of the following and explain the sound in writing as if it were part of a story.

- an airplane
- a songbird
- a busy downtown street
- a forest in the fall with leaves underfoot

_____

_____

_____

_____

_____

Choose a place where you and a friend can sit and listen to the sounds around you. Close your eyes for at least five minutes and listen to your surroundings. What kinds of sounds did you hear? (City sounds? Human sounds? Animal sounds? Sounds in nature, such as the wind?) Where were the sounds? (Near you? Far away? Up in the sky?) What did the sounds tell you? (Someone is approaching? There is a lot of traffic? A storm is coming?)

Describe the sounds you heard in writing. Try to make the reader *hear* exactly what you heard and *feel* exactly as you felt.

Name _____ Date _____

Touch!

Describing how something feels when you **touch** it helps a reader to understand what you're writing about. The sensation of touch communicates many signals and feelings. Telling how something feels in your hands can help describe your emotions. For example, here are some words to describe what you touch and how it makes you feel.

hot — pain   slimy — yucky   soft — good   bumpy — strange

Hold something in your hands with your eyes closed. Then make a list of words describing what you felt when touching the object. Write a paragraph that details what the object felt like and the emotions brought on by touching it. Do not reveal what the object is until the end of your paragraph. Leave it up to the reader to guess what it is.

_____

_____

_____

_____

_____

_____

Describe objects only by touching them. Have your friend choose an item to place in your hands. With your eyes closed, say words that come to mind as you feel the item. For example, if you held a quarter, these words might come to mind: small, metallic, hard, ridges on the edges, round, raised design, and cold to touch. Your friend will write down the words. Without opening your eyes, guess what the object is. Do this with several items. Then give your friend some items to identify, while you do the recording.

Name _____ Date _____

Ah, the Aroma!

Everyone enjoys it when the aroma of something we love comes wafting our way. The smell of bread baking often draws us in as we pass by bakeries. As the scent of coffee brewing floats through the air, coffee lovers are enticed into coffee shops. And who can resist the lure of the aroma of popcorn when entering a movie theater?

Our noses also inform us when something is displeasing. Passing a garbage dump, a barnyard, or a sewer may prompt us to quickly close the windows of our car, or to pinch our noses.

Like all of our senses, the sense of smell can trigger emotions. The scent of someone's perfume can remind us of a person we love and instantly take us back to the last time we were with that person. A smell we dislike can also trigger the memory of a bad experience.

Describing smells and the emotions they bring out in a character gives your reader a better sense of your character or a scene. Here is an example:

> Benita paused as she passed by the rose garden. The overpowering sweet scent of the flowers beckoned her. She stooped down and lifted a lovely pink rose to her face. Its perfumed scent surrounded her, and a smile came to her face as she remembered her grandmother's beautiful garden. For a moment, she was lost in time, remembering her grandmother's gentle voice and the wonderful times they spent together.

Now try writing your own paragraph about a character's feelings about a smell.

Ask a friend to hold an object under your nose for you to smell. With your eyes closed, sniff it and describe what you smell and your feelings about the smell for your friend to write down. Make a guess about the identity of the object. Do this with several objects. Then pick some objects for your friend to smell and describe, while you do the recording.

0-7424-1784-0 *After School Writing Activities*

Name _____ Date _____

Stars Danced in the Sky

Personification means giving human qualities to animals or objects. Underline all of the examples of personification in the paragraphs below.

Example: The <u>leaves skipped and danced</u> down the city sidewalks.

1. Every autumn, the farmers' market bustles with activity. Pedestrians swarm the farmers' stalls. An abundance of fruit and vegetables from the fall harvest crowd the tiny stalls. Now that the wind breathes a chill into the air, everything must be picked from the fields and orchards. The stalls are dressed with corn stalks, scarecrows, and pumpkins. Scents from the apple cider, hot dog, and peanut vendors beckon the shoppers. The street is alive with throngs of people enjoying the sights and sounds of market day.

2. Autumn chills the air and soil, releasing the warmth that sustained us through the summer months. Trees wear their brightest colors. It's as if the leaves are attending a ball as they swing, swirl, and waltz slowly toward the ground. When the last of the leaves are still able to dance, winter blows in and sings a different song.

Write your own descriptions to personify each object or animal. Remember, to personify means to give them human qualities.

3. a rushing river
4. the breeze on a summer day
5. a race car
6. an animal

Write a paragraph about a thunderstorm using personification. Have a friend do the same and combine your paragraphs to create a story.

0-7424-1784-0 *After School Writing Activities*

Like Distant Drums

A **simile** compares two things using the words *like* or *as*. These words clearly show that a comparison is being made.

Examples:　The thunder boomed like distant drums.
　　　　　　　My pillow is as fluffy as a cloud.

A. Write a word from the Word Bank on the lines below to complete these similes.

sky	ice cube	kangaroo
tiger	sun	prune

1. Martina's new overalls were as blue as the _____.

2. At the track meet, Stefano sprang off the starting line like a _____.

3. Max's toes were as cold as an _____ after sledding all day.

4. Artis jumped like a _____ in the sack race.

5. The spotlight in the theater shot beams of light on the actors as bright as the

_____.

6. After soaking in the bathtub, my sister's skin looked like a _____.

B. Complete the following similes. Try to think of colorful comparisons.

1. She was as delicate as a _____.

2. Juan felt as cool as a _____.

3. Mr. Peron growled like a _____ when his car wasn't fixed on time.

4. Yesterday it was as hot as _____.

5. The storm last night was like a _____.

6. My brother dances like a _____.

Write a paragraph describing one of the following situations using similes. Ask a friend to write one too and find the similes in each other's paragraphs.

the cafeteria during lunchtime　　　　　a summer picnic
waking up from a nightmare　　　　　　a day at the amusement park

Name _____ Date _____

My Brother Was a Prince

A **metaphor** compares two things <u>without</u> using *like* or *as* by using a word or phrase which means one thing to describe another.

Examples: My brother was a prince for picking me up after the game.
No one predicted that the storm would be such a monster.

Read each sentence below. Circle the letter of the sentence that most clearly tells what the metaphor means.

1. The stars were diamonds in the midnight sky.
   a. The stars were big.
   b. The stars were shining.
   c. The stars were brilliant and sparkled in the night sky.

2. Arnaud was a tiger on the prowl.
   a. Arnaud was growling with anger.
   b. Arnaud was wearing my striped pajamas.
   c. Arnaud was very quiet and sneaky.

3. After being grounded for a day, Cecilia felt like her room was a prison.
   a. Cecilia was forced to stay in her room all day.
   b. Cecilia didn't like going out.
   c. Cecilia didn't like her room.

4. I was struck dumb when my teacher asked me a question.
   a. I forgot how to talk when my teacher asked me a question.
   b. I couldn't speak a word when my teacher asked me a question.
   c. I was angry when my teacher asked me a question.

Write your own metaphors with a friend for two of the items below. Combine your sentences to create a paragraph about the subject.

a man who works very slowly   a stingy person
a spring day   an old, worn-out car

0-7424-1784-0 *After School Writing Activities*

Name _____ Date _____

Clearly Confused

An **oxymoron** is a phrase which contains words that are opposite in meaning but when put together result in a different idea. Using an oxymoron creates good imagery in both stories and poems.

Examples: Tony was <u>clearly confused</u> by the instructions.
I took a <u>big sip</u> of my root beer float.
The salesman said the diamond ring was a <u>genuine fake.</u>
Our teacher told us that the banana peel left on the floor was a <u>safety hazard.</u>

Underline the oxymorons in the sentences below.

1. It was awfully nice of my aunt to take me to Chicago.
2. There was only a dim light in the hallway of the apartment building.
3. The iguana that floated by on an inner tube was pretty ugly.
4. Once again our basketball team won the game.

Write a sentence for each oxymoron below.

all alone   terribly pleased
second best   small crowd
certain risk   act naturally

_____

_____

_____

_____

_____

Work with a friend to think of an oxymoron to describe your bedroom, your classroom, a brother or sister, and a pet, if you have one.

Name _____ Date _____

Strong as an Ox!

A **hyperbole** is an extreme exaggeration used for emphasis or to create a special effect in writing.

Example: My backpack weighs a ton!

Write an **H** if the sentence is a hyperbole. Otherwise, leave the line blank.

_____ **1.** I am so hungry that I could eat a horse!
_____ **2.** My dad is as strong as an ox.
_____ **3.** Antoine is so smart.
_____ **4.** That hole is so deep it goes straight through to China.
_____ **5.** Ramone can run faster than anyone I know.
_____ **6.** I jumped so high that I hit my head on the moon.
_____ **7.** We scared Mrs. Bradshaw to death.

Write your own hyperboles, or exaggerations, for these sentences.
Remember to write in complete sentences.

8. I was thirsty. _____

_____

9. George's bedroom was clean. _____

_____

10. Michelle's sandwich was big. _____

_____

11. I was late. _____

_____

Read a tall tale with a friend. How many hyperboles did you find in your story?
Write your own tall tales. Remember to use hyperboles.

Name _____ Date _____

Ribbit

Onomatopoeia (ON-uh-MOT-uh-PEE-ya) is the use of words that imitate natural sounds. Using these words makes writing more interesting.

Examples: All you could hear at night in the campground was the **crackle** of the campfires.

My brother made a big **splash** when he jumped into the pool.

Read these sentences. On the lines, write the words that are examples of onomatopoeia.

1. The tornado whirled over the lake. _____

2. The woods were so quiet, we could hear a twig snap. _____

3. The windows rattled as the hurricane got closer to shore. _____

Underline the words in this selection that sound like their meanings.

4. The marsh behind Kitty's house is filled with sound. Toads and tree frogs ribbit at nightfall. Sometimes the chirping of the crickets drowns out the sounds of the little frogs. But the croak of the big bullfrogs can always be heard. Each bird has a unique song, too. There are blaring caws, gentle whistles, and cheery trills. Even the buzz of mosquitoes can be heard in the marsh. I don't know how Kitty sleeps with all that racket going on!

Visit the zoo or a farm with a friend. Write paragraphs about your trip using at least six words that show onomatopoeia.

Name _____ Date _____

Blast! Roar! Crossword

Synonyms are words that have the same or nearly the same meaning.

Fill in the blanks with synonyms of the verbs listed below.
To help you along, some of the letters have been given.

Across

1. desire	20. placed
4. trample	21. matured
7. tilt	24. sparkled
9. loan	27. hurry
12. spoke	28. throw
14. lift	30. fibs
15. fasten	32. carries
16. awaken	36. capture
19. mimics	37. explode

38. mistake
39. haul
40. decay
41. love
42. frighten
43. caught
44. scan
45. operate

Down

1. strolls	15. disembark
3. rob	17. lubricate
5. labored	18. foam
6. encounter	22. obtain
7. halt	23. break
8. intertwined	25. dined
10. escape	26. tap
11. fantasize	27. sleeps
13. tow	28. phone

29. frightens
30. bait
31. presses
32. rip
33. arrange
34. trampled
35. talk
36. allege

0-7424-1784-0 *After School Writing Activities*

Name _____ Date _____

Comes and Goes

Antonyms are words that have opposite meanings.

Fill in the blanks with antonyms of the words listed below.
To help you along, some of the letters have been given.

Across

2. more	**27.** few
5. dry	**28.** daughter
8. fast	**31.** women
11. below	**33.** in
13. off	**35.** wrong
16. morning	**39.** disobey
17. cries	**41.** disown
20. yes	**43.** talker
21. borrowed	**44.** sink
22. know	**45.** live
23. bad	**46.** fierce
24. go	**47.** dry
25. him	**48.** crooked
26. she	

Down

1. pa	**24.** accept
2. hated	**26.** cold
3. odd	**29.** later
4. received	**30.** us
5. weak	**31.** your
6. well	**32.** old
7. tender	**34.** over
9. lad	**36.** busy
10. lost	**37.** stay
12. above	**38.** fat
14. all	**39.** young
15. smaller	**40.** west
18. host	**42.** came
19. villain	**44.** land

0-7424-1784-0 *After School Writing Activities*

Name _____ Date _____

Thesaurus

A **thesaurus** is a valuable tool for a writer. It's a book that contains synonyms (words that mean the same) and antonyms (words that mean the opposite). Many words have similar but slightly different meanings. A thesaurus can help a writer determine what he or she wants to say in exactly the right way.

All of the words in the Word Bank show different meanings of the word *good*. For each sentence, write the word from the Word Bank that replaces the word *good*.

Word Bank				
decent	sizable	beneficial	pleasant	undamaged

1. Mr. Duncan is a good man. _____

2. My grandma won a good amount of money at the bingo game. _____

3. The sailors said there was a good wind today for the race. _____

4. It was so good to see my old friend on Saturday. _____

5. Even though they threw my peach in the bag at the grocery store, it was good. _____

Look up *good* in a thesaurus and find other synonyms that could be used in the sentences above.

Look up these words in a thesaurus. Have a friend do the same. Write sentences using a synonym for each word. Look at the different ways you can express yourself starting out with the same words!

bad   happy   sad   darkness   light

Name _____ Date _____

Chuckled

When writing dialogue, a writer often uses the word *said* before or after someone speaks. Using more descriptive action verbs can help to bring a story or poem alive. Look at the sentences below using the word *said* and then compare them to the same sentences with more descriptive verbs.

"I am hungry," said Juan.

"I want tacos," said Julieta

"I am hungry!" exclaimed Juan.

"I want tacos!" shouted Julieta.

"Let's go pick up some food," said Papa.

"Okay," said everyone.

"Let's go pick up some food," suggested Papa.

"Okay!" everyone agreed.

On the lines below, write four verbs you could use in this sentence instead of cried. The first one has been done for you.

My sister <u>cried</u> when she fell off her bike.

_____ wailed _____

_____

_____

_____

_____

In each sentence below, only the verb has been changed. Choose one of the examples and write a paragraph using that sentence.

"Well, I'll be," chuckled Uncle Bert.

"Well, I'll be," sighed Uncle Bert.

"Well, I'll be," whispered Uncle Bert.

"Well, I'll be," shouted Uncle Bert.

Using dialogue, write a short conversation you had recently with a friend or member of your family. Ask your friend to do the same. Exchange paragraphs and work together to see how many descriptive verbs you can come up with to replace the ones you've both used.

Name _____ Date _____

Widely Grinned

Adverbs and **adverbial phrases** tell *how*, *when*, or *where* something happens. They can be a single word, such as *now*; a word formed from an adjective by adding *ly*, such as *slowly*; or a group of words. Adverbial phrases begin with a preposition. Using them helps the reader to "picture" what you are writing about. Here are some examples:

I walked <u>quickly</u> <u>down</u> <u>the</u> <u>path</u>.
He left <u>at</u> <u>noon</u> to meet Danielle <u>at</u> <u>the</u> <u>park</u>.
Eduardo was shouting <u>loudly</u> <u>with</u> <u>his</u> <u>friend</u> in the bleachers <u>at</u> <u>the</u> <u>soccer</u> <u>match</u>.

Adverbs can answer more than one question in a sentence. Complete the following sentences by writing adverbs or adverbial phrases that answer the questions in parentheses.

1. The jack-o'-lantern was _____.
(where?)

2. Ghosts were flying _____ _____.
(where?) (how?)

3. The skeletons danced _____ _____.
(how?) (when?)

4. We trick-or-treated _____ _____.
(how?) (where?)

5. The horror sounds CD screeched _____ _____.
(how?) (when?)

Adverbs are also used to tell exactly how something is said when using **dialogue** in writing. For example:

My sister <u>frightfully</u> screamed, "The ghost has disappeared!"

Make up a conversation between you and a friend on Halloween. Work together to add adverbs to the dialogue to show *how* you said things.

Name _____ Date _____

Animal Expressions

There are many animal words or expressions you can use to help liven up your writing. Match the expressions below with their meanings by writing the letters on the blanks.

____	**1.** crocodile tears	**a.**	pretend to be asleep or dead
____	**2.** stool pigeon	**b.**	a short nap
____	**3.** guinea pig	**c.**	to play
____	**4.** catnap	**d.**	to tell on someone
____	**5.** eager beaver	**e.**	bothers you
____	**6.** to rat on	**f.**	a decoy or informer
____	**7.** hold your horses	**g.**	suspicious
____	**8.** play possum	**h.**	foolish person
____	**9.** clam up	**i.**	someone anxious to do something
____	**10.** get your goat	**j.**	shy, embarrassed
____	**11.** monkey around	**k.**	fake crying
____	**12.** sheepish	**l.**	terrific
____	**13.** the cat's meow	**m.**	wait patiently
____	**14.** fishy	**n.**	to be quiet
____	**15.** a bear	**o.**	something really difficult
____	**16.** turkey	**p.**	someone who tries something first
____	**17.** quick as a rabbit	**q.**	fast

Work with a friend to write sentences using the animal expressions above to describe people you know.

Name _____ Date _____

The New World

The order or **sequence** of sentences is very important in some paragraphs. **Transition words** help to show the sequence of the sentences.

Before Christopher Columbus left on the voyage that led to his discovery of the New World, he had many things to do. The events leading up to his journey are numbered below in the correct order. Choose transition words from the box below to write these events into a complete paragraph. The topic sentence is written for you.

1. He studied maps and thought he could sail west to Asia.
2. He asked the king of Portugal for ships, but the king refused to help Columbus.
3. He asked for a royal commission from Spain for ships, but they would not help him.
4. In 1492, King Ferdinand and Queen Isabella, rulers of two Spanish kingdoms, gave him the ships he needed for the voyage.
5. Columbus set sail for Asia, but he discovered the Americas instead.

Christopher Columbus had many things to do before he could begin his journey.

Transition Words
Finally,
Another,
First,
Often,
Second,
One,
Next,
Then,
Once,

_____

_____

_____

_____

_____

_____

_____

_____

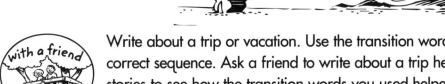

Write about a trip or vacation. Use the transition words to put your trip into the correct sequence. Ask a friend to write about a trip he or she has taken. Trade stories to see how the transition words you used helped you feel as if you were on one another's trip.

Name _____ Date _____

The Tipsy Tugboat Tooted Its Horn

Consonance is a consonant sound repeated anywhere in a series of words.
Example: Dr. Lemke **d**elivered an a**d**orable boy.

Alliteration is a beginning consonant sound repeated in a series of words.
Example: Fireman **F**redo **f**ought the **f**ire on the corner of **F**ranklin and **F**remont.

Assonance is a vowel sound repeated anywhere in a series of words. Remember that vowels and combinations of vowels can make more than one sound.
Example: The pi**e** flew high in the sk**y**.

Read each sentence. Write on each line whether the sentence is an example of consonance, alliteration, or assonance. Underline the letter sound or sounds that are repeated.

1. _____ Six swans swam by.

2. _____ The tipsy tugboat tooted its horn as it tossed in the waves.

3. _____ Mr. Reilly really wanted to ride on a roller coaster.

4. _____ Helene sighed when I replied that we couldn't look for shells in the rising tide.

5. _____ Two taxi drivers tackled the thief.

Write your own sentences using consonance, alliteration, and assonance. Have a friend do the same. Then exchange sentences and write a paragraph based on each sentence.

Name _____ Date _____

All the King's Horses

Quotation marks show a character's exact words. Put quotation marks outside of the punctuation that is included in the quote. Capitalize the first word of the quote, unless the quote is a partial sentence. Separate a quotation from the rest of the sentence with a comma, question mark, or exclamation point.

Examples: "Humpty Dumpty sat on the wall. Humpty Dumpty had a great fall. All the King's horses and all the King's men," the child recited, "couldn't put Humpty together again."

"Nature wears one universal grin," stated Henry Fielding.

Add the correct punctuation to these quotations.

1. Benjamin Franklin said Early to bed and early to rise makes a man healthy wealthy and wise

2. I am always doing that which I can not do in order that I may learn to do it Pablo Picasso stated

3. All sorrows can be borne if you put them into a story or tell a story about them Isak Dinesen, the Danish author wrote

4. All for one and one for all wrote Alexandre Dumas, the French dramatist. It was the Musketeers' motto in *The Three Musketeers.*

Go with a friend to the library and take out books that include conversation. Notice the quotation marks while you're reading. Copy a conversation from the book without using any quotation marks or punctuation. Have your friend do the same and switch papers to correctly place the marks.

Name _____ Date _____

"Oh, My!"

A **dialogue** is a conversation between two or more characters. Reading what a character says reveals much about the character and the situation.

Read this dialogue between Mrs. Murphy, Kate's mother, and Ms. Bosgraaf, Kate's teacher.

"Kate's always been a good girl," Mrs. Murphy said quietly.

Ms. Bosgraaf scowled before she spoke. "I've been annoyed by Kate's behavior this week. She brought ten white mice to my classroom on Tuesday. It made math class impossible."

"Well, scientists often use white mice."

"Not during math tests, Mrs. Murphy." The teacher's dark eyes blazed. "Replacing the cook's sugar with salt in the lunchroom, however, was the last straw!"

Think about what you've learned about the characters. Then, continue the conversation on the lines below.

_____

_____

_____

_____

Write dialogue for the situation below or make up your own situation. Discuss the situation with a friend and carry on a conversation as you imagine your characters would. Then, write the conversation down.

A discussion between two squirrels about which park is the best in town.

 0-7424-1784-0 *After School Writing Activities*

Name _____ Date _____

Writer's Toolbox Crossword

A **literary device** is a tool the writer uses to make a story more descriptive so the reader can *see* what is happening.

Each clue is a tool or technique a writer can use. Read each clue and use the literary devices in the Word Bank to complete the puzzle.

Across

2. I'm so hungry that I could eat a horse!
7. She was as gentle as a summer breeze.
9. told in the first person
11. This would not be the last time.
12. Five fine frogs fished for fun.

Down

1. Hal had a happy hamster.
3. Gene turned thirteen on Halloween.
4. The cardinal chirped high up in the tree.
5. His voice was like a big base drum.
6. The wind howled.
8. She heard the eerie sound again that night.
10. humorous, serious, sad, jubilant

Word Bank

simile	hook
foreshadowing	hyperbole
point of view	personification
metaphor	consonance
onomatopoeia	alliteration
tone	assonance

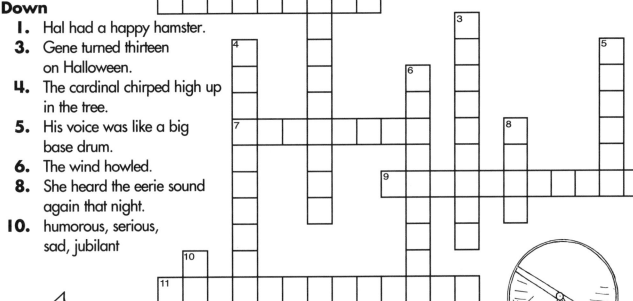

Name _____ Date _____

The New Kid

Narrative writing tells a story. Use a **story map** to plan a story.

Plan a story by making a story map from these ideas. Write the ideas into the plan where they fit best.

- First, Mr. Brunswick introduced me to the other kids in the class.
- beginning of fourth grade
- Then, one courageous girl said she'd show me around the school.
- Mr. Brunswick, the class, and me
- Finally, other kids welcomed me to Seattle and Hillcrest Elementary School.
- Hillcrest Elementary School
- My family moved to Seattle this summer. I'm the new kid here.
- Next, some of the kids teased me about my southern accent.

Story Map

1. **a.** setting: _____

   b. characters: _____

   c. problem: _____

   _____

2. first event: _____

_____

3. second event: _____

_____

4. third event: _____

_____

5. resolution: _____

_____

Write a story about the new student using the story map above. Have a friend write a story using the same story map. Read each other's stories and see how they're different.

Name _____ Date _____

Bigfoot

Outlining is a good way to keep your information and paragraphs in order or sequence when you are writing. If you outline, you can plot the sequence before you write. This makes writing a story much easier.

Below is some information about the Bigfoot or Sasquatch mystery. List each fact under the proper heading in the outline that follows.

- Bigfoot has brownish fur, looks like half-man, half-ape, and is up to or over seven feet tall.
- In 1967, a Bigfoot was caught on film by Roger Patterson in northwest California.
- The man-like creature may simply be a large bear.
- Human-shaped tracks were discovered from 12 inches to 17 inches long.
- When bear tracks in snow melt, they may look like huge footprints.
- Cultural histories of Native Americans include many stories and beliefs of a hairy, man-like creature.
- There have been several expeditions and sightings.
- Bigfoot walks erect on thick legs.
- Bigfoot lives in wilderness areas of North America, especially the Pacific northwest.

I. What is it?
   A. Appearance _____
   B. Where is it found? _____

II. Does it really exist?
   A. Evidence
      1. _____
      2. _____
      3. _____
      4. _____
   B. Explanations
      1. _____
      2. _____

with a friend

Get together with a friend and pretend you have found the huge tracks of a Bigfoot in the woods. Based on the outline above and your imagination, write a story together about your experience.

 0-7424-1784-0 *After School Writing Activities*

Name _____ Date _____

First... Next... Then...

In order to do anything—make a sandwich or give your dog a bath—you have to carry out a number of steps in the right order, or **sequence**. Words like *first*, *next*, *then*, and *finally* help show the sequence.

Here is a list of steps for making a papier-mâché pumpkin. They are not in the correct sequence. Write them in the correct order on the lines below.

1. When the newspaper is dry, cut out a hole in the bottom, burst the balloon, and paint it orange.
2. Dip the strips of newspaper into the mixture.
3. Cut out a face for the pumpkin.
4. Apply the strips to the balloon.
5. Blow up a round balloon and tie the end.
6. Mix two parts water with one part flour.
7. Stir until the mixture is smooth, sticky, and wet.

First: _____

Next: _____

Then: _____

Fourth: _____

Fifth: _____

Sixth: _____

_____

Finally: _____

Write instructions with a friend for doing the following—making an ice-cream sundae, making a paper airplane, or doing a cartwheel.

0-7424-1784-0 *After School Writing Activities*

Name _____ Date _____

Walfredo and the Cat

The **plot** is the plan, or series of events, in a story. The **events** in the story are often attempts made to solve the main character's problem. Often there are added troubles for the main character. The events build to a **climax**, which is the point of the most forceful action in the story. It comes right before the end of the story, which is called the **resolution**.

Read the problem. Then, circle the paragraphs that might be part of the story's action.

1. **Problem:** Walfredo is supposed to play the saxophone at the Mouse King's Ball, but he has to get past the cat first.

   a. Walfredo built a paper airplane to fly off the kitchen counter and over the cat. He was too heavy and the plane crashed. Walfredo had to run for cover!
   b. The next day, the Mouse King sent soldiers to arrest Walfredo.
   c. A dog began to bark when a car drove past the house.
   d. Walfredo practiced the saxophone for many years.
   e. The King once gave Walfredo a new saxophone.
   f. Walfredo hummed lullabies, trying to get the cat to fall asleep. The cat yawned but never fell asleep.
   g. Walfredo shot some rubber bands at the cat, but the cat did not move.
   h. The cat had made many attempts to catch the clever mouse, but the cat had only come close to catching him.
   i. Walfredo flicked the kitchen lights to send a message to the Mouse King. The king sent soldiers to distract the cat.

2. Choose the best climax for this story. Remember, the climax has the most forceful action.

   a. Walfredo gets caught by the cat, but the Mouse King's troops rescue him and he plays at the ball.
   b. Walfredo waits so long for the cat to fall asleep that he misses the ball.
   c. Walfredo runs past the cat but is too late to play the saxophone at the ball.

Write your own climax idea for this story and have a friend write the resolution.

Name _____ Date _____

Developing Characters

Before creating fictional characters, it helps to **observe** real people. Being a good observer helps you to become a good writer. The little things about someone or something are often the details that bring the story to life for the reader.

Observation is a two-step process. First, the writer takes notes on what he or she is observing. Later, those notes are used to create paragraphs. Below are notes taken during the observation of someone in a park. With Step 1 completed for you, go on to Step 2 and write a paragraph about this person based on the notes.

Step 1: Notes
boy in the park—nine or ten years old—tall and skinny—white T-shirt—blue-jean shorts—watch on left wrist—buzz cut, brown hair—red, high-top tennis shoes—carrying a bouquet of flowers—running slowly—drizzly day—doesn't seem to notice rain

Step 2: Paragraph _____

_____

_____

_____

_____

_____

_____

_____

_____

_____

With a friend, choose someone to observe. Take separate notes, then use your notes to each write a paragraph. Exchange your paragraphs. Note the differences in your observations and how you used them to write your paragraphs. Work together to combine your paragraphs and expand them into a story.

Name _____ Date _____

Describing Characters

Describing a character's appearance, qualities, and actions paints a picture for the reader.

Read this description of Ichabod Crane from *The Legend of Sleepy Hollow.*

> He was tall but exceedingly lank, with narrow shoulders, long arms and legs, hands that dangled a mile out of his sleeves, feet that might have served for shovels, and his whole frame hung together most loosely. His head was small and flat at top, with huge ears, large green glassy eyes, and a long snipe nose, so that it looked like a weathercock perched upon his spindle neck…

—Washington Irving

Describe a real or fictional person's appearance and qualities. Character qualities show what a person is like, such as brave, nervous, intelligent, proud, nice, or mean. Use the following list to record important details.

Face: _____

Hair: _____

Size: _____

Clothes: _____

Gestures and Movements: _____

Qualities: _____

Using the details you wrote down for the character above, work with a friend to describe this character in one of the following situations. Be funny or true to life.

- the power has gone out during a thunderstorm
- a dinner at a fancy restaurant or a truck stop
- someone's first visit to a farm or a big city
- a train or subway ride

0-7424-1784-0 *After School Writing Activities*

Name _____ Date _____

A Day in Your Life

You can write about a character using different **points of view**. Here are some examples.

Scenario 1 (character talking to self):

What's that awful noise? Is that a tornado siren? No, wait a minute. It's that pesky alarm clock! Can it be time to get up already? It's 6:00 A.M.

What day is this? Friday? Yes. Oh, good. There are parent-teacher conferences today, so I don't have school. I can sleep in. Yes!

Scenario 2 (third person—as though someone was watching and writing):

She woke to the sound of a siren. Sleepily, she pulled the covers back over her head and shrunk under them moaning, "I'm too tired to get up right now."

Suddenly, a hand reached over her and the noise stopped.

"You don't have school today, honey," her Mom whispered. "There are parent-teacher conferences, so you can sleep in."

Scenario 3 (first person—the author is telling the story):

My day begins with the sharp, terrifying noise of the alarm clock. More like a tornado siren than anything else, but there is no escaping its message. Time to get ready for school. The day has begun.

Write about someone getting ready for school. Try writing it from each of the points of view above.

Write about a day in your life and ask a friend to write about the same day in his or her life. Choose one of the points of view above to start your story. Remember to take your reader through each part of your day, helping him or her to see, feel, smell, and taste everything you do. Read each other's stories.

Setting the Scene

When and **where** a story takes place are important decisions for the writer. Will it be a murder mystery at a hotel? Will it be an adventure story at a ranch? Will it take place in an art museum, in a wagon train, or on a spaceship?

The story's setting helps to express the mood of the story. In order to paint the scene, a writer needs to experience it. That is why many writers research or travel to places they wish to write about.

Here is an example of describing a setting using the two-step process of observation (notes at the scene) and writing.

Step 1: Notes

late afternoon—hot sun suspended over the mountains—mountains cast in shadows of purple and blue—horses grazing in the foothills, swatting flies with their tails—birds chirping and fluttering about in the nearby trees—far-off bark of a dog—the air is still—heavy, sweet scent of orange blossoms and jasmine fills the air

Step 2: Paragraph

As she walked toward her horse's stall, Moria drank in the heavy, sweet scent of orange blossoms and jasmine that filled the still, late afternoon air. She stopped for a moment to watch the purple and blue shadows on the mountains beyond. The sun, still hot, was suspended above them, as if placed there. She gazed out at the horses grazing in the foothills, lazily swatting at flies with their tails, and listened to the birds chirping and fluttering about in the trees. Far off, she heard the bark of a dog at play. It was a beautiful place, this California.

Write your own story beginning. Remember to show **when** and **where** the story takes place so readers will understand your setting.

With a friend, go to a place that you would like to use as a setting for a story. Spend some time there, paying close attention to what you *hear, see, smell, taste,* and *feel.* Each take your own notes and write your setting descriptions later. Exchange your descriptions.

Name _____ Date _____

Grabs Your Interest

The beginning of a paragraph often **leads** the reader into the story by stating an interesting fact or asking an exciting question. Read the paragraph below. Choose the best lead and write it on the line. It will be the first sentence of the paragraph.

- Pyramids are very large buildings in Egypt.
- Pharaohs had large pyramids built for their tombs.
- For 4,300 years, the Great Pyramid of Khufu at Giza was the tallest building in the entire world.

1. _____

When it was built, the pyramid was about 480 feet (146 m) high and was 751 feet (229 m) on each side. It had more than two million stones, each weighing more than two tons. The pyramid was the tomb of the great Egyptian pharaoh, King Khufu. The pyramid held his mummy and the treasures that the Egyptians believed he would need on his journey into the afterlife. Though no longer the tallest building, Khufu's tomb, the Great Pyramid of Giza, is still the largest stone building on earth.

The very beginning of a story can also be a **hook**, which grabs the interest of the reader and makes the reader want to finish the rest of the story.

Example: The wind screamed, tossing aside trees and fences as it went.

Read each hook below. Circle the letter of the question that it will most likely make the reader ask.

2. The night was too quiet and too dark. They should have heard some owls, a distant wolf, or at least the constant buzz of crickets.
   a. Who are they?
   b. Why was everything so quiet?
   c. Where was the moon?

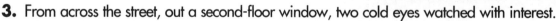

3. From across the street, out a second-floor window, two cold eyes watched with interest.
   a. Was the street in a big city?
   b. What kind of building was across the street?
   c. Who was watching what?

Look through magazines and newspapers with a friend to find hooks and leads in the very beginning of articles. Did they make you want to read the article?

0-7424-1784-0 *After School Writing Activities*

Name _____ Date _____

Tornado Warning!

A **topic sentence** expresses the main idea in a paragraph. A **lead** prompts the reader to read more about the topic. **Supporting sentences** explain more about the main idea. A paragraph often includes at least three key supporting sentences.

Read each topic sentence below and circle three sentences that support each topic.

1. Tornadoes form as a destructive whirling wind with a funnel-shaped cloud when warm air and cold air meet.
   a. They form when the two air masses come together.
   b. States in the Great Plains often have storms.
   c. Warm air rises from the ground, and the storm winds begin to swirl in the sky.
   d. A tornado is extremely dangerous.
   e. Tornadoes over water are called waterspouts.
   f. When the swirling wind reaches down to the ground, it is called a tornado.

2. Tornado Alley is made up of states in the center of the United States from north to south.
   a. States with mountains do not have many tornadoes.
   b. Tornadoes can form quickly.
   c. The states in Tornado Alley have open, flat land and many storms.
   d. Tornadoes are likely to occur every year in this part of the country.
   e. A tornado warning is issued when a tornado is sighted from the ground or seen on radar.
   f. Texas, Oklahoma, Kansas, and Nebraska are all part of Tornado Alley.

3. A tornado touched down very close to our house last spring.
   a. The sky turned dark, even though it was daytime.
   b. Weather forecasters do not know exactly when a tornado will occur.
   c. Tornadoes sound like trains.
   d. We could hear the tornado rumble past our windows.
   e. My aunt once saw a tornado while she was driving.
   f. The high winds knocked down our neighbor's tree.

Name _____ Date _____

And She Lived Happily Ever After

The **theme** is the subject or overall message of a story.

Read the short summaries of the stories below. Choose one of the **themes** from the list that best matches each summary. Write the letter of the theme on each line.

Themes

a. Honesty is the best policy.

b. Believe in yourself.

c. Good things eventually happen to those who are kind and good.

_____ **1.** Once there was a girl who lived with her stepmother and stepsisters. Although the girl was kind, they were cruel to her. One day, her fairy godmother rewarded her goodness by helping her go to the royal ball. There, she met a prince and fell in love.

_____ **2.** Once Joey took a small apple from a fruit stand. He knew it was wrong, but he didn't have enough money, and he really wanted the apple. The next day, he went back and apologized to Mr. Chin, the owner of the stand. Mr. Chin was a kind man and understood. He gave Joey a job after school so he not only could pay for the apple, but also earn money for his family.

_____ **3.** The boys asked Alfonso to join their basketball team. The only problem was that Alfonso didn't know how to play. First, he told the others he was sick. The next time they asked him, Alfonso said his family was going somewhere. He was embarrassed that he didn't know how to play. Finally, he couldn't hide it anymore. The others taught Alfonso to play, and it turned out he was a great player. He had worried for no reason at all.

Go to the library with a friend and take out books of fairy tales. After you both read a few stories, discuss the theme of each fairy tale. Use the theme of your favorite fairy tale to write your own short story.

Name _____ Date _____

The Title Is Vital

The **title** is a very important part of a story. It should give a hint about the subject of a story, but it should not give away the ending.

Example: *What the Moon Saw*

The first word, the last word, and all of the important words in a title are capitalized. When titles are printed in books or articles, they are in italics, *like this*. When you write a title, underline it.

In a book: *The Ugly Duckling*
When you write it: <u>The Ugly Duckling</u>

Pick the best title for this passage of a story. Remember, a good title doesn't give away too much.

1. The summit appeared several feet away. Mario's feet ached from supporting his weight on the tiny ledge. Suddenly, his brother's face emerged just above him. Pedro let down the rope to Mario and pulled him to safety. Together, they triumphed over the wall of granite known as White Mountain.

    a. *Triumph Over White Mountain*   **c.** *Challenging the Mountain*
    b. *Mario and Pedro*   **d.** *Safe Mountain Climbing*

Write a title for the passage below.

2. _____

The rope weakened as the impressive, wild horse labored against his tether. When he reared and struck down at the rope with his hooves, the rope broke, releasing him. Untamed and free, this beautiful creature galloped across the rich, brown soil. With his nostrils flaring, he breathed in the smell of freedom.

Write new titles for your favorite books with a friend. Write a title for a book about the history of your city or town. Write new names for yourselves. How did you decide what the titles and names would be?

Name _____ Date _____

Hoot!

Foreshadowing is hinting or offering clues to the reader about what will happen in the story.

Example: During the hayride, we heard the hoot of an owl off in the distance. We were all laughing and having such a good time, we didn't think anything of it at the moment. (This hints that something unexpected will happen.)

In each paragraph, underline the words or sentences that make you think that something might happen. Then write on the lines what you think will take place.

1. Penny had rehearsed her lines over and over again for the school play. Boy, was she surprised when the play ended.

_____

_____

_____

2. Everyone was already on the bus for the field trip to the science museum. Ryan looked pale and the teacher asked him if he felt sick. Ryan told her he felt fine. Actually, he felt a little sick to his stomach, but at the time, he thought it was nothing to worry about.

_____

_____

_____

3. Ynez could run faster than anyone in her class. No one expected what happened in the park after school.

_____

_____

_____

Write a story beginning with a hint about what might happen. See if your friends can guess what is going to happen next in your story.

Name _____ Date _____

Mrs. O'Leary's Cow

A **paragraph** is a group of sentences that tell the reader about one main idea. If sentences do not support the main idea, they do not belong in the paragraph.

Read each paragraph below and circle the letter of the sentence following the paragraph that tells the main idea. Cross out one sentence in each paragraph that does not support the main idea.

1. Most people know that Chicago is called the Windy City. People have many ideas about how Chicago got this nickname. Some say that it's because a group of people bragged about the city constantly to try to get Chicago chosen as the site for the 1893 World's Fair. People in cities chose school boards, too. A newspaper editor wrote that people shouldn't believe all the claims of "that windy city." Now you know one possible reason why Chicago is called the Windy City.

   a. Chicago is called the Windy City because people bragged about it so much.
   b. Editors who write about windy cities run their newspapers like businesses.

2. Chicago is well known for the great fire that that swept through the city in 1871. It burned for three days and destroyed about one-third of the city. The homes of more than 90,000 people burned down and more than 250 people lost their lives. Fires cause a lot of damage all around the world. No one knows exactly how the fire started. Some people think Mrs. O'Leary's cow kicked over a lantern. Then the lantern started a fire behind someone's house. Because of a long dry spell, the fire spread quickly and grew into the fire that became part of Chicago's history.

   a. A cow started the great fire of 1871.
   b. The great fire of 1871 destroyed a large part of Chicago and many people lost their lives.

With a friend, look up a story about an event in the history of your city or town. Using the same lead sentence, each write supporting sentences to describe this event and combine them to create a story.

Name _____ Date _____

Wrapping It Up

A paragraph may have a **concluding sentence** at the end of the paragraph. It reminds the reader of the main idea and wraps up the supporting sentences, giving the reader something to think about or asking a question.

Circle the letter of the best concluding sentence for these paragraphs.

1. Polar bears have everything they need to survive in the frozen Arctic. First, they do not feel the cold like humans do. Their black skin absorbs heat, and their hollow hairs shield their bodies from the cold. Second, these marine bears are good swimmers. They have wide feet and stiff hairs on their legs to push against the water. Finally, they have learned how to hunt in the snowy, white Arctic. Polar bears cover their black noses with their paws while they hunt.

    a. Polar bears eat seals, fish, bird eggs, and other food.
    b. There are no other bears that could live so well in the frozen world of the Arctic.
    c. Their fur can turn yellowish in the summer.

2. Other people have pets they love, but my dog, Sasha, is the sweetest dog on earth. She never barks at me. She only barks at strangers, which makes her a good watchdog. Another reason Sasha is great is because she is nice to other dogs. She never growls, and she stays by my side during our walks. Finally, Sasha always comes when I call her. She runs like the wind to get to me, and then sits so I can pat her on the head.

    a. I feel so lucky to have such a good dog for a pet.
    b. Sasha is very smart, and she learns tricks easily.
    c. I think dogs make the best possible pets.

Write a paragraph about your favorite animal in the zoo. Ask a friend to write about his or her favorite. Do some research on the Internet or at the library about your animals. Don't write a concluding sentence for your paragraphs. Trade paragraphs and write the concluding sentence for each other's paragraph.

Name _____ Date _____

Welcome to the Show!

A **descriptive paragraph** gives information or explains something by painting a picture in the reader's mind. Using all five senses—*sight, sound, smell, taste,* and *touch*—to describe something makes a paragraph more interesting.

Write down the sense—sight, sound, smell, taste, or touch—that best describes each thing. Then write words or phrases to show how that sense describes it. The first one is done for you.

thing	sense	description
1. chocolate caramels	taste, smell	sweet, chewy, sugary, delicious
2. orchestra		
3. audience		
4. spotlight		
5. theater seats		
6. costumes		
7. perfume		
8. dancer		

with a friend

Write descriptions of things you've seen or experienced at a theater. Ask a friend to write about his or her own experience. Remember to "paint a picture" for your reader by using different senses. Compare each other's stories.

Name _____ Date _____

Mystery at the Museum

Make a sentence more interesting by **adding details** and **explanations** to tell *how, when,* or *where* something happens.

Detective Cage is asking the people in the museum questions. Help him by circling the sentences that give the most details and explanations he needs to solve the case. (Hint: the correct sentences the detective needs must tell how, when, and where.)

Nature Museum

Basic sentence: Detective Cage searched the museum.

Adding how: Detective Cage searched the museum carefully.

Adding when: Detective Cage searched the museum carefully for two days.

Adding where: Detective Cage searched every room and office of the museum carefully for two days.

1. Where was Mr. Malinski when the keys disappeared?
   a. Mr. Malinski was cleaning a glass case with a cloth.
   b. Mr. Malinski was in the Gem Room wiping a glass case.
   c. Mr. Malinski spent ten minutes in the Gem Room wiping a glass case with a cloth.

2. What was Mrs. Rockwell doing when she noticed her ring was missing?
   a. Mrs. Rockwell was at her desk cataloging gems.
   b. Mrs. Rockwell was in her office cataloging gems after lunch.
   c. Mrs. Rockwell worked in the Gem Room until late at night.

3. Where was Muriel when her rock was taken?
   a. Muriel first found her rock when she was on a tour of Spain two years ago.
   b. Muriel spent two hours at a lecture in the Rock Room learning about geodes.
   c. Muriel was busy learning about geodes for two hours.

Write four more questions with a friend that would help Detective Cage find out how, when, or where the thefts happened.

Name _____ Date _____

Missing Ring

Make a sentence more interesting by telling why something happens. This allows a reader to understand the **cause** and **effect.**

Basic sentence: Mr. Malinski put his keys on a table.
Better sentence: Mr. Malinski put his keys on a table
so he could clean a glass case.

Write the cause and effect from each sentence on the lines.

1. The ring, piece of quartz, and keys were stolen when they were left out in the open.

2. When Mrs. Rockwell, Muriel, and Mr. Malinski discovered their items were missing, Mr. Malinski called Detective Cage to ask for his help.

3. Detective Cage wanted to solve the crime so he looked for clues.

4. Detective Cage found out who took the missing ring because he found an important clue.

Cause   **Effect**

1. _____   _____

   _____   _____

2. _____   _____

   _____   _____

3. _____   _____

4 _____   _____

   _____   _____

   _____   _____

Work with a friend to create your own crime scene. Make a list of causes and effects.

0-7424-1784-0 *After School Writing Activities*

Name _____ Date _____

Solving the Case

You can make your sentences more interesting and informative by telling *who, what, where, when,* and *how.*

Regular sentence: Muriel walked into the room.
Super sentence: Muriel, the museum's rock expert, walked slowly into the meeting room early that morning to discuss the case with Detective Cage.

Detective Cage shared his findings with the people at the museum. Each of his sentences is missing one of the basic elements: *who, (did) what, where, when, why,* or *how.* Cross out each boxed element when you see it in the sentence. One word will be left.

1. Mr. Malinski, the manager of the Nature Museum, gently set his keys on a table in the Gem Room because he needed to clean one of the glass cases with a cloth.

who	did what	where	when	why	how

2. Mrs. Rockwell, the manager of the Gem Room, set the ring on her desk before lunch because she was going to show it to her coworkers.

who	did what	where	when	why	how

3. Muriel, the museum's rock expert, hunted carefully for two days, trying to find her missing piece of quartz.

who	did what	where	when	why	how

4. The naughty thief, who loves shiny objects, left clues in each room during the crimes because this species of thief sheds every season.

who	did what	where	when	why	how

Write your own interesting and informative sentences with a friend to explain *who, what, where, when, why,* and *how* the keys, ring, and piece of quartz were taken by the thief.

Name _____ Date _____

Showing How You Feel

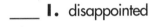

Tone is the writer's attitude or mood about the subject or topic. The writer's tone can be funny, serious, persuasive, happy, and so on.

Match each sentence to the tone it expresses.

____ **1.** disappointed   **a.** That's why we should all work hard to conserve energy.

____ **2.** happy   **b.** My projects never win at the science fair even though I work so hard on them.

____ **3.** funny   **c.** Every country on earth should do everything they can to prevent pollution.

____ **4.** serious   **d.** I can't believe I got an Honorable Mention!

____ **5.** technical   **e.** After I glued part A onto part B, I inserted the cotter pin.

____ **6.** persuasive   **f.** The first time I tried this, I ended up with spaghetti in my hair!

Circle the letter of the word that describes the tone of the paragraph below.

7. I never quite know what to do when teachers tell us we are going to have a science fair. First, they say we need to pick a project. The good experiments like exploding volcanoes and twisting tornadoes were all done last year. So what's left? Then, they make us do research. That means a trip to the library and filling out those index cards with our research, which always get mixed up. Couldn't we just use notebook paper? Then, there's the display. Playing soccer is easy, but doing a science project is hard. The science fair makes me a wreck!

     a. funny   **b.** serious   **c.** persuasive   **d.** frustrated   **e.** happy

Discuss with a friend what mood you'd like to set in a story. Using a subject that you've both experienced, write a paragraph using words that set the tone and have your friend do the same.

     0-7424-1784-0 *After School Writing Activities*

Name _____ Date _____

Putting It All Together

All of the words in the Word Bank are important elements that you use in writing. Complete the crossword using these words.

Word Bank

transitions
plot
hook
point of view
resolution
beginning
middle
end
dialogue
setting
climax
characters
title
conflict

Across

6. the last part of a story
7. shows who is telling the story
10. gets the reader's interest
11. highest point of action
12. events leading to a climax
13. how a story starts
14. people, animals, or things that do or say something in a story

Down

1. words used to show the order or relationship of events
2. the body of the story
3. the name of the story
4. how the problem is solved
5. the problem or difficulty
8. where and when the story takes place
9. characters talking in a story

Choose a book that both you and a friend would like to read. As you each read it separately, identify all of the story parts. When you've both finished reading, discuss the conflict. How was it resolved? What was the climax?

Name _____ Date _____

My Stories

No matter how old you are, there are experiences in your life that would make interesting stories. You may have had a wonderful friend who moved away. You may have owned a pet with a special talent. You may have had a bad scare or a thrilling adventure. You may have visited a special place that you would like to write about. Things you like to do or do not like to do also make good themes for personal narratives.

Personal narratives tell about your experiences. To write a compelling personal narrative, you need to choose an unforgettable experience or an event that made an impression on you. Personal narratives are fairly short and describe only one experience.

The personal narrative below is from *Black Beauty*. It is written from the horse's point of view.

> There were six colts in the meadow besides me. I used to run with them and had great fun; we would all gallop together round and round the field. Sometimes we had rather rough play, for we would frequently bite and kick.
>
> One day, when there was a good deal of kicking, my mother whinnied to me to come to her, "I wish you to pay attention to what I am about to say. The colts who live here are very good colts, but they are cart-horse colts, and, of course, they have not learned manners. You have been well-bred and wellborn; your father has a great name in these parts, and your grandfather won the cup two years in a row at the Newmarket Races; your grandmother had the sweetest temper of any horse I have ever known, and I think you have never seen me kick or bite. I hope you will grow up gentle and good and never follow bad ways. Do your work with goodwill, lift your legs up high when you trot, and never kick or bite, even in play."
> —*Anna Sewell*

Write about a Christmas or other holiday that was very special for you and why it was special. Include what people said to you in quotations just as Black Beauty's mother did in the passage above.

Brainstorm ideas with a friend about what memorable experiences you've had. Choose one experience to write about. Be sure to include your thoughts and feelings about the event or persons involved.

Name _____ Date _____

Writing a Biography

A **biography** is the story of a person's life. It contains significant facts about a person's life. The facts are often used to form an opinion and conclusion about the person.

Think of someone you know and admire that you would like to write a biography about. It could be someone in your family, a friend, or a neighbor. On a separate sheet of paper, write down the answers to the following questions about this person. Combine your answers to write a biography and conclude from your answers why you admire this person. Is this person good, honest, intelligent, kind?

1. Where and when was this person born?

2. What were the family and home of this person like?

3. Where did this person go to school?

4. What jobs has this person had?

5. What special interests, hobbies, sports, or crafts does this person enjoy?

6. What interesting things have happened to this person?

Discuss with a friend someone you both admire and would like to write a biography about. Answer the questions above and combine your answers. Based on your answers, write several sentences that tell the facts and your opinions about this person.

Name _____ Date _____

Writing an Autobiography

An **autobiography** is the story of your life that you write yourself. You can tell the entire story of your life or just the main events. No matter how long you make it, your autobiography should be interesting and communicate what makes you a unique person.

To help get you started through the journey of your life, answer the following questions on a separate sheet of paper.

1. What is your name?

2. What do you like to be called?

3. Where were you born?

4. Where do you live now and where have you lived before?

5. What school do you go to and what other schools have you attended?

6. What is you favorite subject? Why?

7. What are your favorite hobbies? Why?

8. What are you very good at doing?

9. How many brothers and sisters do you have?

10. Who are your friends and why are they special to you?

11. What are your dreams for your future?

12. What makes your family different from other families?

13. What are you grateful for in life?

Write descriptive sentences from your answers including important events and major influences. Combine these into a story about your life.

Share your autobiography with a friend and discuss how your lives have been different.

 0-7424-1784-0 *After School Writing Activities*

Name _____ Date _____

And So, My Fellow Americans...

Speeches inform others about a topic and/or persuade them to view things in a certain way. We often think of speeches when we think of people running for political office, such as the President of the United States. Political speeches are only one type of speech, however. Any time a person must speak in front of a group, he or she must prepare a speech.

The **purpose** of the speech must be clear for it to be effective. Are you trying to encourage people to vote for you? Are you trying to explain a cause that you believe in and have researched? Are you trying to convince people that it is important to save the whales?

Once you have your purpose in mind, you can build your speech around it using examples, reasons, steps, important statistics, a series of questions, a short history, or funny stories that show your point.

Begin and end your speech by clearly stating your **major point**. Below are the last two paragraphs from John F. Kennedy's Inaugural Address on January 20, 1961. Look up and read this speech on the Internet or in the library. What do you think the main point of the speech is?

And so my fellow Americans... ask not what your country can do for you... ask what you can do for your country. My fellow citizens of the world... ask not what America will do for you, but what together we can do for the Freedom of Man.

Finally, whether you are citizens of America or citizens of the world, ask of us here the same high standards of strength and sacrifice which we ask of you. With a good conscience our only sure reward, with history the final judge of our deeds; let us go forth to lead the land we love, asking His blessing and His help, but knowing that here on earth God's work must truly be our own.

— *John F. Kennedy*

Name _____ Date _____

And So, My Fellow Americans...(cont.)

It is also very important to think about who your **target audience** will be. Write your speech so this audience will understand it. Avoid using any words or ideas that *this* audience wouldn't understand.

The **time limit** of your speech may be determined by your audience or by the subject of your speech. Avoid being too wordy and dragging the speech on because your audience may lose interest. An effective speech requires a careful choice of words and needs to be direct.

Below is the first paragraph from Lincoln's Gettysburg Address, given November 19, 1863, on the battlefield near Gettysburg, Pennsylvania. Look up and read this speech on the Internet or in the library. Who do you think Lincoln's target audience was and why do you think his speech wasn't very long but was still so effective?

Four score and seven years ago, our fathers brought forth upon this continent a new nation: conceived in liberty, and dedicated to the proposition that all men are created equal.

—*Abraham Lincoln*

Write a speech that you would give if you were elected president of your class.

Do some research with a friend on endangered animals. Choose an animal that interests you and write speeches to convince someone why this animal should not disappear from the planet. Give your speeches to each other, to friends, and family. Remember that speeches are meant to be heard, so they must sound good as well as be well written. Have your friend turn away from you when you give your speech as if you were giving your speech on the radio. See what your friend thought about how it sounded.

Why I Should Keep Morgan

In a **persuasive paragraph**, the writer tries to persuade the reader to do something or to think in a certain way.

A kitten follows you home from the park. Your mother has some worries about keeping the kitten. Read the reasons she's worried and circle the letter of the sentence that might persuade your mother that keeping the kitten won't be a problem.

1. "You cannot keep the kitten because she might belong to someone else."
   a. I will put up "Found" signs around the neighborhood to see if someone recognizes her.
   b. She does not have a name tag or a collar, and she followed me home.
   c. I already named her Morgan.

2. "You cannot keep the kitten because you do not know how to take care of her."
   a. You can take care of her, and I'll just play with her.
   b. Taking care of a kitten is easy.
   c. I'll go to the pet store and ask them how to take care of a kitten.

3. "You cannot keep the cat because it will make the whole house smell."
   a. She does not smell any worse than my brother's shoes.
   b. I will spray the house whenever she smells bad.
   c. We can put a litter box for her in the basement, and I'll clean it every day.

Write a persuasive paragraph telling a parent why you should be able to keep a lost kitten. Use the sentences above to deal with his or her doubts and add your own reasons. Remember that a paragraph needs a topic sentence and a concluding sentence.

Think of a place you'd like to go on a vacation with a friend and your family. Write a persuasive paragraph with your friend telling why you both think you should go there.

0-7424-1784-0 *After School Writing Activities*

Name _____ Date _____

Volcano Erupts!

Scientists often write descriptions of what they observe. They use words that give the most complete description possible.

Circle the best description of each insect.

1.

a. This bug has a black body.
b. This insect has two wings, large eyes, six legs, and a black body.
c. This insect can fly.

2.

a. This insect has antennae.
b. This bug can walk.
c. This insect has six legs, small eyes, and long antennae.

Pretend that you are scientists in Hawaii. A volcano has erupted on the other side of the island. You have gone to see it from a safe distance and observe what has happened in the air, on land, and in the sea.

Do some research with a friend about volcanoes on the Internet or at the library. Write a few sentences together about what your observations would be if you saw a volcano erupting. Be sure to describe how it looks in the air, on land, and in the sea.

0-7424-1784-0 *After School Writing Activities*

Name _____ Date _____

A Good Book

Have you read any good books lately? Or have you read one in the past year that was unusual, interesting, or exciting? When we discover a wonderful book, we like to share our opinions about it.

On a sheet of notebook paper, write the name and author of a book that you have read and enjoyed. Answer the following questions to organize your ideas. Your answers will help you write a **persuasive book report.**

1. What is the main idea, focus, or theme of your book?

2. Who is the central character of the book? How would you describe the physical, mental, and emotional characteristics of this person?

3. Are there other important characters in the story? Who are they and what do they do?

4. What makes this book so interesting or exciting?

5. Give one example of a scene that was outstanding. Write some of the details.

6. Who tells the story in the book, or who is the narrator?

7. What is the narrator's point of view? What can the narrator see and hear?

Write a report about the book you selected, using the information from your answers. The concrete details and specific examples in your answers will enable you to write a persuasive report about your book.

Look through newspapers and magazines with a friend to find book reviews. Read the reviews, then discuss how the questions above were answered.

0-7424-1784-0 *After School Writing Activities*

Name _____ Date _____

You're the Movie Critic

Whether you have been to the movie theater or rented a video to watch on television,

all of us today are **movie critics.**

Think about a movie you have seen recently. How would you rate it? Was it a great movie? Or was it

just okay? Or maybe you thought it was really bad. How many stars would you give it—four, three, two,

or one?

Write a movie review telling what you liked and didn't like about the movie. Was

it exciting? Did it make you laugh out loud or make you cry? Was it scary?

Where did the story take place? Who were the main characters? What was the

movie about? Would you recommend it to others? What was your favorite part of

the movie?

Have a friend write a review about the

same movie, then exchange your reviews

to see if you had the same opinion.

Discuss the things you both liked and

disliked about the movie.

0-7424-1784-0 *After School Writing Activities*

Name _____ Date _____

The Reporter's "Five and One" Rule

All good **news reporters** follow the "Five and One" rule. "Five" refers to *who, what, when, where,* and *why.* The "one" refers to *how.* Answers to these questions provide clear information that can be quickly understood in a newspaper or a news report on television.

Study this first sentence from a paragraph of a made-up newspaper sports article. *When she was young, the champion, Sarah Hughes, worked hard to perfect her skill in ice skating because her dream was to win a gold medal at the Winter Olympics.* All of the questions are answered in one sentence.

Write your own article, using the "Five and One" rule. Select a famous star, hero, or expert in the subject you have chosen. Answer the following questions.

1. Who is the star, hero, or expert you have chosen?

_____

2. What does he or she do?

_____

3. When did he or she begin to do the activity that made him or her famous? You can add any other detail. _____

_____

4. Where was he or she born? Where does your person perform his or her activity? Where did he or she learn to be outstanding? _____

_____

5. Why is this person different or outstanding? Why does your person like the activity? Why do you admire your person? _____

_____

6. How did your person become famous? How does your person rank among others?

_____

_____

Write an article about a person or something that happened in your own town. Have a friend do the same and exchange stories. Check each other's story to make sure the "Five and One" rule questions were answered in the story.

Name _____ Date _____

Breaking News!

The facts in a **news story** answer the questions *who, what, when, where,* and sometimes, *why.* Read this news story.

Farmer Spots UFO

Sioux City, March 30—Thaddeus Briggs of Lone Pine Farm reported seeing an unidentified flying object in his corn field last night around 9 P.M. He described the UFO as a round object surrounded by a very bright white light. It hovered about 50 feet off the ground, emitting eerie sounds for about five minutes, and then sped off to the north.

"It was really a peculiar sight. I wasn't exactly frightened—just startled," Briggs stated.

1. On the lines below, fill in the facts from the news story above.

Who: _____

What: _____

When: _____

Where: _____

_____

Newspaper reporters state only the facts of a story. A reporter may use an opinion or feeling if it is a quotation. Quotations are the exact words spoken by people.

2. Are there any opinions given in the story above? Write the opinion below and underline the expressive words used in the opinion.

_____

_____

Name _____ Date _____

Farmer Spots UFO

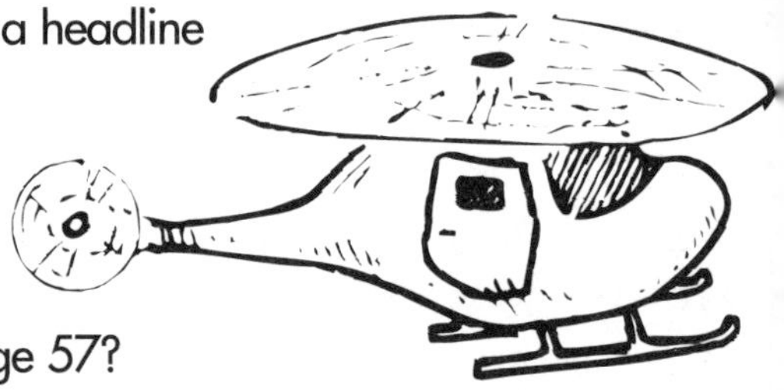

Headlines state the main idea of a story in a few words. Here is a headline from the March 31 Sioux City paper.

Disc Jockey Plays Music from Helicopter

Does this headline give you an idea for the *why* of the story on page 57? If so, fill in the reason below.

Why: _____

_____

The first paragraph of a news story is called the **lead**. The lead gives the important facts of a story. The lead should also be interesting and well written, so a reader will continue to read the news story.

Write a lead paragraph for the Sioux City headline above. Make up specific facts that explain *who, what, when, where,* and *why*.

_____

_____

_____

_____

_____

_____

Write a news story based on one of the headlines below or make up a headline. Have a friend do the same.

New Science Museum to Open
Hunter Finds Strange Footprints
Tropical Storm Moves Inland

Use a good, factual lead paragraph that answers the "Five W" questions. Try to include a quotation that states an opinion. Read each other's stories. Check to see if *who, what, when, where,* and *why* were answered in the story.

Name _____ Date _____

Writing Ads for Products

Think of some of the most popular consumer products on the market today. Why are some brands of toothpaste, tennis shoes, soda pop, canned soup, fast foods, computer games, and types of music more successful than others?

What makes a product desirable to the general public? When marketing a product, advertising professionals ask *what is the purpose* of the product, *who* will want to buy it, and *why* people are going to want it. Then **advertisements** are created to sell the product.

One part of successful advertising is writing slogans that say the most with the fewest words.

Invent a product that you would use almost every day, something you would really enjoy. Think of something you think you need, such as a food, drink, tool, piece of clothing, accessory, or something fun, like a game. Perhaps you can think of a totally new product you would buy if you could.

What would it be?_____

What is the purpose of the product? _____

_____

Who will want to buy it?_____

Why are they going to want to buy it? _____

_____

Write a slogan for this product that says the most using the fewest words.

Example: Have it our way. Our burgers taste better.

When you're watching television with a friend, pay attention to the **jingles** in commercials. *(A jingle is a song with a catchy repetition.)* Pick your favorite jingle in a commercial and try to come up with a new one for the same product.

Name _____ Date _____

My Favorite Holiday

Everyone looks forward to holidays when family and friends get together for special traditions, food, and fun.

What is your favorite holiday? _____
Explain why you selected this holiday by writing down the events that take place during your favorite holiday.

How long is your favorite holiday or holiday season?

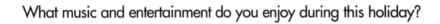
_____

What music and entertainment do you enjoy during this holiday?

_____

What kind of clothing or costumes do you wear?

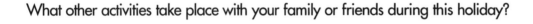
_____

What kinds of food are served during this time?

_____

What other activities take place with your family or friends during this holiday?

_____

Write a few paragraphs based on these answers to explain why this particular holiday is so special for you. Be **descriptive** with your details. Paint a picture with words so the reader can see, hear, and smell this holiday time.

Think of one memorable experience during your favorite holiday. It could be something like when you got a new bike for Christmas, when your favorite aunt traveled across the country to be with you for Thanksgiving, or the year you won the Halloween costume contest. Ask a friend about his or her special moment during a holiday. Write stories describing your special moments.

0-7424-1784-0 *After School Writing Activities*

Name _____ Date _____

Thinking of You

Receiving a **greeting card** always makes you feel appreciated. Greeting cards are popular during holidays and other special occasions, and the surprise of getting a card for no particular occasion at all is especially nice.

Think of someone who would enjoy getting a special greeting from you.

What is the person's name? _____

What things has this person done that you appreciate? _____

_____

_____

_____

What has your special person done or said that affected you? _____

_____

_____

_____

Write a two- to four-line note to the person you chose. Include the nice things you listed above. When you finish, use a blank greeting card or a piece of note paper folded in half. If you use note paper, find an image in a magazine that you like and glue it on the front, or draw or paint a picture. Copy your lines on the inside and send it to your special person.

_____

_____

_____

_____

_____

_____

0-7424-1784-0 *After School Writing Activities*

Today I...

A **journal** or a **diary** is a daily record of personal experiences and observations. People write both facts and opinions in their journals. Read the following example. Underline the sentences of fact and circle the sentences of opinion.

Tuesday...

Today was pretty lucky. On the way to school, I found a dollar. I think it must have fallen out of somebody's pocket. I took it to the school office. The secretary told me that if nobody claimed it, I could have it at 3 o'clock. Finally 3 o'clock arrived. I felt nervous when I went into the office. The secretary smiled and handed me the bill, saying, "Nobody claimed it." I felt great. On the way home I bought two comics.

For one week, write a journal entry each day about what you did after school. Remember to write the day and date each time you write in your diary.

with a friend

Discuss with a friend what each of you has done in the last seven days. Pick one day where you spent part of it with each other. Where were you? What did you do? Each write a journal entry that tells four facts and opinions about that day. Compare your accounts of that day.

The next time you go on a family trip or a field trip with your class, keep a journal of the events of the trip and your feelings during it.

Name _____ Date _____

Writing a Letter to a Friend

In a letter to a friend, you may include a **heading**, which shows the writer's address as well as the date. The **greeting** states who you're writing the letter to, and the **body** presents your message. The **closing** is the way you say goodbye. Your **signature** tells the person receiving the letter who wrote it. In a letter to a friend, you usually only use a first name in the greeting and the signature. Below is a sample of a letter to a friend.

Tuesday, June 28

Dear Sergio,

It was so good to see you at the park the other day. It's been such a long time since I've seen you. I've missed all of my old friends since my family moved. Have you seen our friend Chris lately? What's he up to?

I'm having a few friends over for lunch next week. Would you like to come? Please let me know. I look forward to seeing you again.

Your friend,

Lee

Write a letter to a friend or someone in your family that you haven't seen in awhile.

Find out if there are any groups or associations in your town that will set you up with a pen pal in another country. Another possibility is to exchange letters with a soldier who is stationed either in this country or overseas. Have a friend sign up too, and you will both enjoy writing to a new friend. You can share ideas as you write your letters and news when you get letters back.

Writing a Business Letter

A business letter is more formal and is written flush left, where the heading, inside address, greeting, body of letter, closing, and signature all begin at the left-hand margin.

The **greeting** is more formal than in a friendly letter, and includes the name and title of the person receiving the letter. If you don't know the name or title of the person, he or she can be addressed as *Dear Sir* or *Dear Madam*, or *To Whom It May Concern*. The greeting is followed by a colon (:). The **closing** is more formal as well. The most common closings are *Sincerely yours, Sincerely, Yours truly*, or *Cordially*. The **signature** usually has the writer's name handwritten beneath the closing, and then printed or typed below that. Below is a sample of a business letter.

222 Hampton St.
New York, NY 95602
September 30, 2002

Emmett & Gray Publishing Co.
41 Smythe St.
Marblehead, MA 46802

To Whom It May Concern:

I have not received the book, *Life in the Ocean*, that I ordered from your company three weeks ago. I would appreciate it if you would let me know when it will be delivered.

Sincerely yours,

Gene Warren

Gene Warren

Write a business letter to a company that makes a food product, telling them why you like it. Follow the guidelines to format your letter. The company's address may be on the label or box.

Write a make-believe letter to a business with a friend. It could be about a certain product that you both like or one that you'd like to complain about.

Name _____ Date _____

Sunset

How do you suppose the sun knows when to set?

_____

_____

_____

Why do you think the sun is often drawn with a happy face?

_____

_____

_____

Why are the colors in a sunset different every time you see one?

_____

_____

_____

Describe a sunset you have experienced.

_____

_____

_____

_____

_____

0-7424-1784-0 *After School Writing Activities*

Name _____ Date _____

What Does the Future Hold?

Can you think of something you are doing today that could have an effect on the future? Describe it.

_____

_____

Describe three things you are helping to change for the better, whether about yourself or the environment.

_____

_____

_____

If you could travel in time, what message would you give to a child living thirty years in the future? Why?

_____

_____

_____

Describe what you think the future will be like in twenty years.

_____

_____

_____

_____

_____

0-7424-1784-0 *After School Writing Activities*

Name _____ Date _____

Digging Up Ancient History

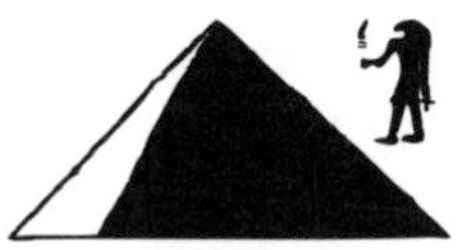

Why do you think the Egyptian pyramids were built?

_____

_____

_____

How do you think the ancient Mayans were able to build the pyramids without

modern equipment?

_____

_____

_____

What do you think an archaeologist would discover digging on the site of a

former Indian village?

_____

_____

_____

What does an archaeologist do?

_____

_____

_____

_____

Name _____ Date _____

All That Jazz

What are three reasons why some people are good musicians and others are not?

_____

_____

_____

Why do you think people enjoy singing with others? _____

_____

_____

If you could master any musical instrument, what would you choose and why?

_____

_____

What do you like most about music?

_____

_____

_____

_____

_____

Name _____ Date _____

I Wish Upon a Star

What do people mean when they wish someone good luck?

_____

_____

_____

What is meant by *superstition?* _____

_____

_____

_____

Why are some things considered to be lucky?

_____

_____

_____

If you had three wishes, what would they be and why?

_____

_____

_____

_____

Name _____ Date _____

Four Seasons

What are the most obvious changes to the environment between summer and winter?

_____

_____

Why do you think some people enjoy warm temperatures more than cold?

_____

_____

Name four activities that are most often done in the winter and four most often done in the summer.

_____

_____

Describe your favorite season of the year and why.

_____

_____

_____

_____

_____

_____

_____

_____

Name _____ Date _____

My Favorite Vacation Spot

Why do many people enjoy traveling to warm climates?

_____

_____

_____

Why do you think so many people like to go to New York City on their vacation?

_____

_____

_____

Describe what it feels like to have nothing to do.

_____

_____

_____

Describe the best place you have ever gone for a vacation.

_____

_____

_____

_____

0-7424-1784-0 *After School Writing Activities*

Name _____ Date _____

How Do You Do?

What are some different ways people say hello to their pets?

_____

_____

_____

How do animals say hello to each other? _____

_____

_____

_____

People have many different ways of saying hello to their family and friends. Give

three examples. _____

_____

_____

_____

Why do many adults shake hands when they say hello?

_____

_____

_____

_____

_____

_____

_____

_____

Name _____ Date _____

Living Longer

Why are people living longer today that they did in the last century?

_____

_____

_____

Why do you think people believe that having a pet helps you to stay healthy?

_____

_____

In what countries do you think people live the longest? Why do you think this is so?

_____

_____

Why do you think most humans live longer than most animals?

_____

_____

_____

_____

_____

_____

0-7424-1784-0 *After School Writing Activities*

Name _____ Date _____

Water, Water Everywhere

What is your favorite thing to do in or with water? _____

_____

_____

Where do rain and snow come from? _____

_____

_____

What would change if we did not have oceans?

_____

_____

_____

Describe ten tasks for which water is a necessity.

_____

_____

_____

_____

_____

_____

_____

0-7424-1784-0 *After School Writing Activities*

Name _____ Date _____

Realistic Fiction

Realistic fiction tells a story that could happen in real life. Read the following paragraphs and cross out the sentences that you don't believe are realistic.

I take the bus to school every day. Nothing much ever happens. Yesterday, however, our bus driver was sick. We had a substitute driver. She wore a dark hat and glasses. I thought she was a government spy.

When I got on the bus, she greeted me in at least 12 different languages! The bus got stuck at the end of my driveway. She got out and picked up the bus and moved it over. A sports car driven by an evil-looking man started chasing the bus. Our bus driver was a good driver. She didn't speed and she didn't drive recklessly. Our bus outran the evil man.

When I got to school, television reporters were there. They wanted to talk to our bus driver. They said she was a film actress who was learning how to be a bus driver for a movie she was making. She didn't talk to any of the reporters, though. She went inside a trailer and refused to come out. The principal came outside and told us we had to go to class.

When I got to class, the teacher took attendance. One student was missing. Her name was Lakeesha. I thought about Lakeesha and how much she looked like the substitute bus driver movie actress. They were the same person!

Think of an event that actually happened to you or someone you know. Now organize the story in the order that it happened. Write a fictional story based on this real event. Remember to include who the story is about, and how, where, when, and why the story happened.

Name _____ Date _____

Science Fiction

Science fiction is a type of fictional writing that imagines what life might be like in the future. The story is an imaginary tale, but there might be parts of it that could be true 25, 50, 100, or more years from now.

Some of the topics you might find in a science fiction story include time travel, space travel, aliens, and the effects of technology. Science fiction writers often choose to set their stories in the future in order to talk about the world in which they live. See if you can tell what issues of today are talked about in the following paragraph.

I woke up feeling sick. My air mask was clogged again. I went to the mask-cleaning station, but I didn't have a $100 bill to turn on the water. I took a breakfast tablet and sprayed Insta-Wash over my body. I opened up a new air mask, put it on, and went outside. I knew it was about noon, because the sun was shining pink through the dark gray air.

Other science fiction writers simply like to create adventure stories that feature rocket ships and other new inventions. These are stories that are meant to entertain, which means that the writer only wants you to enjoy the story. The following paragraph is an example of a science fiction story meant to entertain.

The sea began to move as if a giant wave was about to break. Melanie and I rowed our boat quickly so our boat wouldn't get swamped. I was rowing so hard my hands hurt when I heard Melanie scream. I looked behind me and saw what had frightened her. Something from the depths of the small lake had risen to the surface. A large, circular metal object was revealing itself to us. Lights flashed around the object's middle. A large mechanical arm came out of the ship—if it was a ship—and extended toward us.

0-7424-1784-0 *After School Writing Activities*

Name _____ Date _____

Science Fiction (cont.)

Other science fiction writers write adventure stories about time travel or future wars. One writer, H.G. Wells, wrote famous books about these ideas. In one book, he imagined what war in the future would be like. He described an imaginary new weapon in such detail that it inspired the first tank. In *The Time Machine*, he explained how traveling through time might be possible. The book's hero invents a device that allows him to travel back in time when dinosaurs were still alive. The Time Traveller also travels far into the future.

"It took two years to make," retorted the Time Traveller. Then, when we had all imitated the action of the Medical Man, he said: "Now I want you clearly to understand that this lever, being pressed over, sends the machine gliding into the future, and this other reverses the motion. This saddle represents the seat of a time traveller. Presently I am going to press the lever, and off the machine will go. It will vanish, pass into future Time, and disappear."

—*H.G. Wells*

Finish the science fiction stories that appear on page 76 or write your own story. Draw a picture to illustrate the story.

Create a scene that takes place in the future. Imagine that you and your friend are adults. What will cars look like? How will the food be different? Will the world be a better place? How? What will be some of the new inventions that you and your friend will use? Here's a sample title for a story: "My Best Friend Is a Robot."

Name _____ Date _____

All the World's a Stage

Drama is a story that is told by actors. The ancient Greeks used drama to tell stories about kings, rulers, and Greek gods. These plays were either comedies or tragedies. A **comedy** is a play that makes people laugh. A **tragedy** is a play with an ending that features the downfall of the hero or heroes. Drama continued in Europe during the Middle Ages. During the Renaissance in the 16th century, English writers like William Shakespeare and Christopher Marlowe wrote many comedies, as well as historical and tragic dramas.

Read the topics of the dramas below and write on the lines if you think they would be a **comedy** or a **tragedy**.

1. _____

Ancient Greek dramas by Aeschylus reflected the belief that the gods were jealous and resentful of human greatness, so they imposed a character flaw on a great person that would bring about his downfall.

2. _____

An old English drama, *Gammer Gurton's Needle,* is about the search for a lost needle, a valuable thing to own if you lived in the countryside in those times. Its characters are good-humored and poke fun at each other.

3. _____

The plots of Latin dramas during the Renaissance were sometimes about young men and women who fell in love, had their love thwarted, and through the help of clever servants, eventually won out over their opponents by some sort of trickery or disguise.

In Italy in the late 1500s, ancient Greek plays were discovered that they thought were actually sung by the actors. They decided to try writing musical dramas too, that came to be known as **opera**. Many of these operas were based on ancient Greek dramas. Operas became very popular in Europe with both rich and poor audiences.

Write your own comedy or tragedy based on the explanations above.

Think of a story that happened to you or someone you know. Write down the events in the order that they happened. Think of some of your favorite songs. Use these songs to help tell your story. You have just written a musical! Now perform your musical for your family and friends.

Name _____ Date _____

All the World's a Stage (cont.)

Dialogue tells the listener much about the characters in a play. In the dialogue below, what do you learn about the characters?

Marty: Hey, wait up!

Bobby: Hurry, I don't want to be late for class. We're having a test, you know. Since I barely passed my other history tests, my parents won't let me try out for the soccer team unless I do well on this test.

Marty: How do you think you'll do on this one?

Bobby: Well, I studied hard and I think I'll do pretty well.

Marty: I sure hope so. You're the best player in our class and we need you.

A playwright usually gives directions on how he or she wants the characters' dialogue to be read. These directions tell the characters' actions or feelings. For example, the first line of dialogue might read like this:

Marty: (rushing up to Bobby and out of breath) Hey, wait up!

Write directions for the following lines of dialogue. Tell how the character should read his lines. Tell how the character is feeling.

Bobby: (_____)
Hurry, I don't want to be late for class. We're having a test, you know. Since I barely passed my other history tests, my parents won't let me try out for the soccer team unless I do well on this test.

Marty: (_____)
How do you think you'll do on this one?

Bobby: (_____)
Well, I studied hard and I think I'll do pretty well.

Marty: (_____)
I sure hope so. You're the best player in our class and we need you.

To understand how a drama is created, ask your parents how they first met. Ask them to remember details about what they said to each other, how they dressed, and how they acted. Write down what you learned using dialogue. Include instructions on how to read it. Tell their story in a way that is realistic. Act it out with your friend.

Seeing with Your Ears

In 1920, Pittsburgh radio station KDKA broadcast election results. A new source of entertainment and news was born. After 1920, hundreds of radio stations were built and thousands of Americans bought radios for their homes.

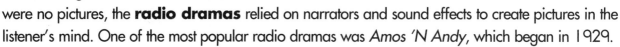

Radio became even more popular when it broadcast a boxing match between Jack Dempsey and Georges Carpentier in 1921. Baseball games were broadcast into nearly three million homes.

As radios became more common, station owners began broadcasting dramas written for radio audiences. Because there were no pictures, the **radio dramas** relied on narrators and sound effects to create pictures in the listener's mind. One of the most popular radio dramas was *Amos 'N Andy*, which began in 1929.

In the 1930s and 1940s, radio enjoyed what is known as its "Golden Age." During this period, radio drama was very popular. Homes across America tuned in every week to hear radio comedies such as *Fibber McGee and Molly* and *The Fred Allen Show*, and dramatic shows such as *The Green Hornet* and *The Shadow*.

Look up a script of one of the old radio dramas mentioned above on the Internet or at the library. Read it and write your own episode for the show following the same format and story line.

Select your favorite story to use as a radio play. Before you begin, bring together all the different items you will need to create your drama's sound effects. Write a script for your radio play. Perform and record your play and "broadcast" it to your family, friends, or classroom. You may want to borrow tapes of old radio drama broadcasts from your local library to help you plan your recording.

Name _____ Date _____

What's That Sound?

When you listen to radio drama, you sometimes need help to imagine what's happening. Writers of radio drama not only put dialogue in the mouths of actors, they also give directions about **sound effects**. For example, you can't bring a car into a studio whenever your radio script says a car horn honked. Instead, you can record a car horn honking or find a small device that makes the same sound.

Sounds tell a listener a lot about what is happening in a radio drama. In radio drama of the past, men and women needed to imitate such sounds as boats, airplanes, and gunshots. Sometimes they used their own voices to imitate animal sounds. Other devices used for sound effects included:

- Wrinkling cellophane to sound like a fire.
- Running a finger along the teeth of a comb to sound like crickets.
- Blowing a straw into water to sound like boiling water.
- Shaking a sheet of metal to sound like thunder.
- Clapping together coconut shells to sound like horse hooves.

After a while, most sound effects were recorded. The tables full of bells, sandpaper, woodblocks, and coconut shells in radio studios disappeared.

Write a short story about something that happened in your neighborhood. Be sure to include all of the sounds you heard. Turn your story into a short radio script with instructions on how to duplicate those sounds.

with a friend

Ask a friend to help you prepare a ten-minute radio script that features original characters or characters from your favorite book or television show. Make sure your script includes plenty of sounds. Bring together all the items you'll need to make the sounds while you read your script to your family or friends. You may also want to use recorded tapes, compact discs, or records of sound effects from your library.

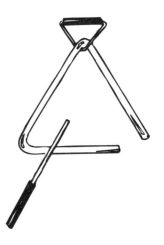

Name _____ Date _____

Red Badge of Courage

The main purpose of **historical fiction** is to give the reader information about a certain time period, person, or event in history. In historical fiction, you can include people who actually lived and have them do things they did not really do or go places where they did not really go. You can make up people and have them do things and go to places that actually existed, or you can make yourself a time traveler and take part in history any way you like!

Read the passage from *The Red Badge of Courage*. Then, answer the questions below.

He lay down on a wide bunk that stretched across the end of the room. In the other end, cracker boxes were made to serve as furniture. They were grouped about the fireplace. A picture from an illustrated weekly was upon the log walls, and three rifles were paralleled on pegs. Equipments hung on handy projections, and some tin dishes lay upon a small pile of firewood. A folded tent was serving as a roof. The sunlight, without, beating upon it, made it glow a light yellow shade. A small window shot an oblique square of whiter light upon the cluttered floor. The smoke from the fire at times neglected the clay chimney and wreathed into the room, and this flimsy chimney of clay and sticks made endless threats to set ablaze the whole establishment.

—Stephen Crane

1. What parts of this passage do you think are historical facts? _____

_____

2. What historical time period do you think is represented? _____

3. What do you think the man in the story does for a living? _____

4. What time period, person, or event from history would you like to write about? Why?

_____

_____

_____

_____

Name _____ Date _____

Red Badge of Courage (cont.)

Writing historical fiction requires some research. Once you decide on what period of history you would like to use in your story, you will need to find out more about the people, the time period, and the events that are connected to your topic.

Here are some important things you might include when you write your story. Make a list using the period of history you've chosen for your story.

- clothing _____
  _____

- ways of communicating _____
  _____

- types of food _____
  _____

- types of houses _____
  _____

- important events of that era _____
  _____

- famous people of that era _____
  _____

- methods of transportation _____
  _____

- ways of speaking _____
  _____

- type of government _____
  _____

Ask a friend to help you choose a person, a place, an event, or a time period of history that you would like to explore. Gather some information for the story from books, films, magazines, or the Internet. Make lists of the information you discover in each of the categories mentioned above. Compose your story together from your lists of information.

0-7424-1784-0 *After School Writing Activities*

Name _____ Date _____

Armchair Critic

Your local newspaper has asked you to be a TV critic. What are your favorite TV shows? Write down why you like these shows. Remember to discuss the characters, the stories, and the acting. What are your favorite episodes and why?

Some things to consider in writing your review:

1. Why do you like this show? _____

_____

2. Are the stories original? _____

3. Are there any other shows like it? What are they? _____

_____

4. What type of audience do you think would like the show best?

_____

Using the answers to these questions, write a review about one of your favorite TV shows.

Watch a rerun of an old black-and-white TV show with a friend and compare it to a new TV show. Keep in mind that you should compare comedies to comedies and compare dramas to dramas. Each of you write down your answers to the following questions on a separate sheet of paper.

1. How are the shows different? How are they the same?
2. Which show did you like better? Why?
3. How has time changed the way TV shows are written? Is this good or bad, in your opinion?

Name _____ Date _____

Lights, Camera, Action!

When you write for television, like writing a play, you have to add **stage directions**. Stage directions describe the setting where the scene takes place and tell the actors what to do or how to say their lines. Stage directions appear in parentheses and are not meant to be said out loud. Here are some examples:

ACT 1, SCENE 1

(A large, messy living room. A couch is covered with books, papers, newspapers, and magazines. BEN and MARJORIE are school students busily preparing for the day ahead. MOTHER sits in an overstuffed chair, watching her children)

BEN: (talking loudly while stuffing his mouth with a donut) Mom! Have you seen my socks? I need my socks! I gotta go to school!

MARJORIE: (sobbing) Mother! You said you'd have my uniform clean for today's big game! And it's not!

MOTHER: (tired but firm) Both of you are teenagers now. You need to handle these problems yourselves.

Some important points to remember when writing your script:

- Realistic dialogue is very important because the characters are telling the story to the audience.
- Dialogue does not have to be in quotation marks because the character is identified at the beginning of each speaking part.
- Remember to imagine your play on stage and write clear stage directions when necessary.
- Acts are like chapters in a book.

Write a new episode for your favorite television show. Before you begin, write down some details about the characters and the settings. Decide what you want your characters to do in this episode. Continue the theme of a recent episode you saw or create a whole new idea.

0-7424-1784-0 *After School Writing Activities*

Name _____ Date _____

Writer in Wonderland

A **fantasy story** is a story that could never happen. Such stories contain events, ideas, or even imaginary worlds that do not, and cannot, exist. Fantasy stories often have magical aspects or include journeys, quests, or dreams. They may have characters such as elves, fairies, leprechauns, wizards, giants, or talking animals. It's fun to write fantasy stories because your imagination can really take off!

The following paragraph from *Alice's Adventures in Wonderland* is an example of a fantasy story.

There was nothing so very remarkable in that; nor did Alice think it so very much out of the way to hear the Rabbit say to itself, "Oh dear! Oh dear! I shall be late!" (when she thought it over afterwards, it occurred to her that she ought to have wondered at this, but at the time it all seemed quite natural); but when the Rabbit actually took a watch out of its waistcoat-pocket, and looked at it, and then hurried on, Alice started to her feet, for it flashed across her mind that she had never before seen a rabbit with either a waistcoat-pocket, or a watch to take out of it, and burning with curiosity, she ran across the field after it, and fortunately was just in time to see it pop down a large rabbit-hole under the hedge.

—*Lewis Carroll*

Imagine what it would be like to...
- travel on stardust
- discover a magical world in a forest
- meet a wizard

Write a fantasy story using one of the ideas above.

Brainstorm with a friend to come up with your own fantasy story. Create the impossible in your story. Have your main character reach a goal, have an adventure, or learn an important truth. Help your readers to escape everyday life by entering your world of fantasy!

Knock, Knock

Everybody knows at least one joke. Below are three different kinds of jokes.

Knock, Knock
Who's there?
Canoe!
Canoe who?
Canoe come out
and play with me?

Silly
Do you know the time?
No, we haven't met yet!

Riddle
How does a boat show affection?
It hugs the shore.

Puns are another type of joke. Puns rely on words with more than one meaning or words that are mispronounced on purpose. The following scene from *Alice's Adventures in Wonderland*, for example, uses puns. The puns are boldfaced.

"When we were little," the Mock Turtle went on at last, more calmly, though still sobbing a little now and then, "we went to school in the sea. The master was an old Turtle—we used to call him Tortoise—"

"Why did you call him Tortoise, if he wasn't one?" Alice asked.

"We called him **Tortoise** because he **taught us**," said the Mock Turtle angrily: "really you are very dull!"…

"And how many hours a day did you do lessons?" said Alice, in a hurry to change the subject.

"Ten hours the first day," said the Mock Turtle: "nine the next, and so on."

"What a curious plan!" exclaimed Alice.

"That's the reason they're called **lessons**," the Gryphon remarked: "because they **lessen** from day to day."

—Lewis Carroll

1. Write down what you think is the funniest joke you have ever heard. Explain what makes the joke so funny.
2. Write your own standup comedy routine. Try to use jokes that everyone can understand.

Obtain a copy of *Alice's Adventures in Wonderland* and act out the Mad Hatter's Tea Party with a friend. Write down what you think makes the scene so funny.

0-7424-1784-0 *After School Writing Activities*

Punch Line

A joke can be a story that is told in a careful sequence. It usually ends with a **punch line**, which is the unexpected twist that makes the listener laugh. Read the comic strip below and pay attention to the order of events.

Name _____ Date _____

Punch Line (cont.)

A. Can you tell the joke on page 88 entirely in words? Write a paragraph about it on a separate sheet of paper. Be sure to write the joke in the correct order of events. Using words such as *then* and *finally* help keep the order clear.

B. If you put the following sentences in sequence, you will get a joke. Number the sentences in order. Then write them in a paragraph. What kind of joke is the punch line in this story? _____

_____ He showed her something that looked like a figurine of a ladybug and said, "This is what I have for collateral."

_____ The loan officer's name was Ms. Patty Whack. When the frog told Ms. Whack that he wanted a loan, she asked if he had collateral.

_____ The bank president said, "Why, that's a knick knack, Patty Whack. Give that frog a loan."

_____ She asked, "Do you know what this is, and should I give him the loan?"

_____ She took it to the bank president and said, "There's a frog out there who wants a loan, and this is what he has for collateral (showing him the figurine)."

_____ A frog went to get a loan at a bank.

Work together to write a joke. Make sure that your story leads up to a funny punch line and that the punch line comes as a surprise.

Name _____ Date _____

Can You Believe This?

A **tall tale** is a greatly exaggerated story. Many times, tall tales feature heroes who accomplish amazing deeds or are responsible for accidentally creating some of the landforms we see today. For example, coyotes raised the tall tale cowboy hero Pecos Bill after he fell off the back of his parents' wagon. Instead of a horse, Pecos Bill was said to have ridden on a mountain lion. He also used a whip that was a live rattlesnake.

Another tall tale character is Paul Bunyan, a giant lumberjack who owned the equally giant Babe the Blue Ox. Paul Bunyan could cut down all the trees in a forest with one swing of his giant axe. Babe would haul all the trees to the river without any help.

Create your own tall tale hero. Make your story funny! Use the following ideas to help you:

1. My tall tale hero is so tall, _____

_____

2. My tall tale hero is so fast, _____

_____

3. My tall tale hero is so smart, _____

_____

4. My tall tale hero snores so loud, _____

_____

5. My tall tale hero can jump so high, _____

_____

6. My tall tale hero is so strong, _____

_____

Let your imagination roam and make up a tall tale about an object, an event, a person, or an animal. Have a friend help you come up with an idea for your tall tale and make a list of exaggerations for your character. Work together to combine them into a story.

90   0-7424-1784-0 *After School Writing Activities*

Name _____ Date _____

Making Fun for Fun

A **parody** is a long joke that makes fun of a story, poem, or song, by imitating it. A parody changes parts of the story or poem to make the reader laugh. For example, a parody of "Mother Hubbard" might have her looking for a bone in the cupboard. She may find the bone, but learns that her dog is on a diet or has become a vegetarian.

A parody of the classic tale of *The Gingerbread Boy* might go something like this:

A poor cobbler and his wife lived in the forest. They had little money and little to eat. The wife baked gingerbread in the shape of a little boy for her husband's birthday. When the gingerbread came out of the oven, the husband said, "What's that smell?"

His wife said, "I'm sorry, dear. I forgot that you don't like gingerbread."

Just then, the gingerbread boy jumped up and said, "Run, run, as fast as you can, but you can't catch me, I'm the gingerbread man."

The husband and wife looked at each other, shrugged their shoulders, and went into the other room to order a pizza and watch television.

Finish the parody of *The Gingerbread Boy*. Remember the other characters he meets in the original story. What other funny things can you make up about him?

Pick a favorite movie, television show, story, or song. Now write a parody of it. Try to make it as funny as you can. Read it to your classmates or family members.

Name _____ Date _____

Myths

A **myth** attempts to explain what is not understood. The ancient Greeks, Romans, and Native Americans invented many myths to explain why things happen. These myths can explain how the earth was formed or why the sun rises in the east and sets in the west.

Read the following myth and answer the question.

When humans first appeared on earth there was only good. Nobody got sick. No one hurt anyone else. Nobody died. Pandora and Epimetheus (EP-i-ME-thee-yus) were two of the first people. They were happy until the god Mercury stopped at their house. Mercury carried a box. He said he was too tired to carry it. He asked Pandora and Epimetheus to keep it for him. After Mercury left, Pandora wanted to see what was in the box. When Epimetheus wasn't looking, she opened it. Out of the box came the spirits of sickness, anger, and sadness. Pandora was very afraid. She rushed to put the lid back on the box. But one spirit remained. It whispered to Pandora to open the box once more, which she did. The one spirit left in the box said its name was Hope, which is the spirit that helps all humans to deal with all the pain and bad feelings in the world.

What does the story of Pandora's box explain?

_____

_____

_____

Write your own myth about something you could not understand without science. For example, you could write about why the moon sometimes shines during the day. Be creative!

Look up Native American myths on the Internet or at the library with a friend. Work with your friend to write your own myths about nature or animals.

0-7424-1784-0 *After School Writing Activities*

Name _____ Date _____

Legends

A **legend** is a story that has been told over the years. Sometimes legends feature people who seem real but who never lived. Robin Hood and King Arthur are two examples of this type of legend. It has never been proven that either of these men existed, but legends about them are the subject of movies, television shows, poetry, and books.

Other legends are about people who really did live. In many of these legends, the truth often is exaggerated. Legends may have changed parts of an original story to include amazing abilities or events. For example, many legends have been told about sports figures such as baseball player Babe Ruth or race car driver Dale Earnhardt.

Before you try writing a legend, look up some legends on the Internet or at the library and read them. In the boxes below, write down the elements that made up the legends.

Person	Remembered For	Special Abilities

With a friend, choose a person from history, sports, or entertainment. Do some research on this person and write a legend about the person's special abilities or accomplishments. Feel free to exaggerate as much as possible to make your legend entertaining.

0-7424-1784-0 *After School Writing Activities*

Name _____ Date _____

The Moral of the Story

A **fable** is a short story that teaches the reader a lesson. The lesson is called the **moral** of the story. The moral is written at the end of the story to make certain the reader understands the lesson that is being taught. The characters in fables are often animals who act like humans. The following is one of Aesop's Fables. It is called *The Lion and the Mouse*.

Once when a Lion was asleep a little Mouse began running up and down upon him; this soon wakened the Lion, who placed his huge paw upon him, and opened his big jaws to swallow him. "Pardon, O King," cried the little Mouse: "forgive me this time, I shall never forget it: who knows but what I may be able to do you a turn one of these days?" The Lion was so tickled at the idea of the Mouse being able to help him, that he lifted up his paw and let him go. Some time after the Lion was caught in a trap, and the hunters who desired to carry him alive to the King, tied him to a tree while they went in search of a wagon to carry him on. Just then the little Mouse happened to pass by, and seeing the sad plight in which the Lion was, went up to him and soon gnawed away the ropes that bound the King of the Beasts. "Was I not right?" said the little Mouse.

1. What is the moral of this fable? Circle it.
   a. Might makes right.
   b. Two heads are better than one.
   c. Little friends may prove great friends.
   d. Don't count your chickens before they're hatched.

2. Explain what the moral of the fable means to you. _____

_____

_____

Write your own fable. Begin by deciding what lesson you want to teach. Invent animal characters to tell your fable.

Name _____ Date _____

Detective Hilary

Read the story below. Then on each line, write a word or phrase that makes sense.

Hilary looked through her _____ at the

_____ street. She thought she recognized the _____ man standing next

to the _____. His face looked like a picture she had seen in the _____. She

went to a _____ booth and put _____ in the slot.

"Sergeant Malaski?" asked Hilary. "It's Hilary. I think I've located your _____."

"What makes you _____ that?" Malaski asked. "We haven't seen him here in

_____. Hilary?"

But _____ had _____. Malaski put down the phone. Hilary was

no longer _____. She was _____ about Hilary's _____.

Hilary had _____ the phone when she saw the _____ looking at

_____. She left the _____ and _____ walked down the

_____. The man _____ her. He wanted to _____ what

Hilary knew.

Hilary found a _____. She asked him if he knew the _____.

The man following Hilary _____. He _____. Hilary was

_____ for now.

 0-7424-1784-0 *After School Writing Activities*

Name _____ Date _____

Monsters in the Basement

Read the story below. Then on each line, write a word or phrase that makes sense.

The laboratory was _____ with blinking _____.

Rudy and Marlena walked down the _____. Bottles of _____ were on

_____ everywhere. Wires and _____ hung from the

_____ and connected to _____. The two _____ were

_____ and walked _____. They were looking for _____.

"Find what you were looking for?" asked Baron Houseman. He wore a _____

and scowled _____ at the boy and girl.

"We were _____" Rudy said. Marlena _____, and said,

"We know that you're _____. We think you're _____ a

_____."

Baron Houseman laughed. "If that were true, do you think I'd let you _____? "

He _____, "I think it's time to..." He was _____ by the

_____ of a large _____. The sound was loud and

_____.

Rudy and Marlena turned around to see _____. Both children held back a

_____ as they _____ away from the _____ that stood

behind them.

"That should _____ hose little _____!" said Baron Houseman.

"They won't be _____ around here any more!"

Name _____ Date _____

Somewhere in the Old West

Read the story below. Then on each line, write a word or phrase that makes sense.

Lily's Saloon was _____. _____ of cowboys and _____ were inside to hear _____ performed by a _____. Many of the men had been _____ a _____ drive for _____. They wanted a _____ meal that Lily _____.

Rascal Dan wasn't _____. He had come to Lily's to _____. Rascal Dan had a _____ named Rattlesnake Jake. Dan and Jake were _____ and _____. Both men were _____ of Lily's cooking.

"Been here long?" Jake _____ Dan.

"Nope," Dan _____. "I've been _____."

"You better _____," said Jake.

"I'm going to _____," _____ Dan.

The two men were _____ by Lily, who _____ them, "You boys better _____."

The _____ men _____ and _____ a _____ table. The _____ began and Lily began to _____ a _____.

Rascal Dan and Rattlesnake Jake didn't _____ Lily's _____. They _____ and the spurs on their _____ _____. Lily _____ tears from her _____ as the two men _____ from her saloon and _____ to the _____ next door for _____.

0-7424-1784-0 *After School Writing Activities*

Name _____ Date _____

Rock 'n' Roll Road Show

Read the story below. Then on each line, write a word or phrase that makes sense.

Bridget was _____. She wanted to _____ her favorite

_____, Mona Lisa's Mustache, for a _____ time. She had learned

to play _____ by listening to _____ by them. Her favorite

_____ was "My Dog Ate My Homework."

Now the _____ was looking for a _____ guitar player. Bridget

hoped that they would _____ her. She _____ for a

_____ before coming to the _____. She also had some new

_____ that she had _____. She thought the band could use some

_____.

When Billy Rand, the _____ player of Mona Lisa's Mustache,

_____ Bridget, he _____. "Good to _____ you,

Bridget," he said. "The band loved your _____."

Bridget _____. She thought it was a good _____ to send the band

a _____ before she _____ them.

Bridget met Wendy Pilgrim, the _____ of the band. "Hey, _____,"

she said, welcoming the young _____. "Let's hear you _____!"

Bridget opened her guitar case and _____ her _____. She

_____ the strings and played the _____ a new song she had written,

"Flowers Chased My Puppy."

 0-7424-1784-0 *After School Writing Activities*

Name _____ Date _____

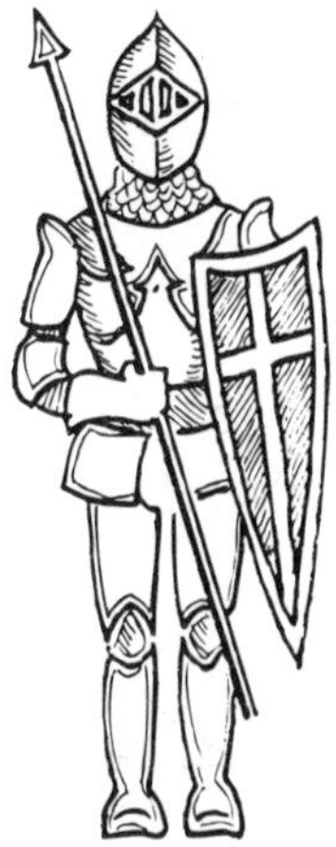

Once Upon a Time

Read the story below. Then on each line, write a word or phrase that makes sense.

King Artie was _____. His _____ had been

_____ by a dragon for a month. Artie's castle was the last place the

dragon hadn't _____.

"Oh, who will _____ us?" asked the _____ king. "Who will stop

the _____ the dragon has _____?"

Not expecting an _____, King Artie was _____ when a voice

_____, "Do not fear, my king. I will save the _____."

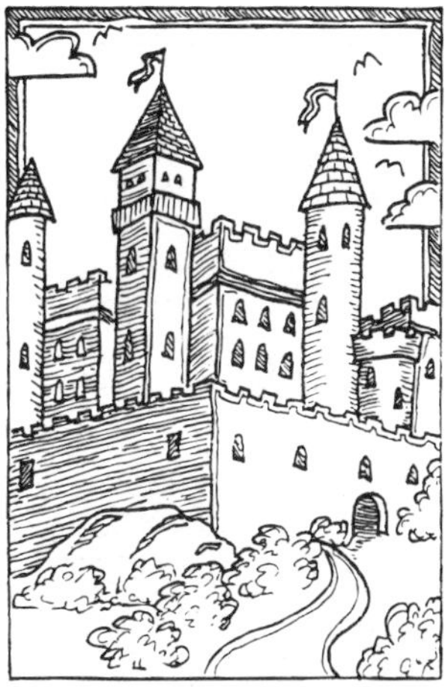

"Who are you?" the _____ king asked.

"I am Rupert the Knight," said the _____.
"I have _____ dragons since I was a _____ boy."

"What is it you _____ to _____

this dragon?" the king asked.

"I am a _____ man," said Rupert. "I never _____ school, and

would like to _____ with the _____ students at your

_____. It would make me most _____ to have an

_____."

Name _____ Date _____

Lost in the Wilderness

Read the story below. Then on each line, write a word
or phrase that makes sense.

I had been hiking all _____ when I _____
I was lost. I had stayed on the _____ until I heard
the river. I thought it would be _____ to fish the
river but did not _____ that it was _____ away.

When I got to the river, I fell _____ on the bank. The ground felt
_____ and I was comfortable. When I woke up, it was _____. I
couldn't find the _____. I was lost!

I tried to _____ what I had been taught in _____ about being
lost in the _____. The best way to _____ is to stay in one place. That
makes it _____ for _____ to find you.

I needed to _____ some shelter to stay warm and _____.
I also took some brightly _____ material from my _____
and tied it to a _____. That way, _____ might see me if
they flew over me in a _____.

Name _____ Date _____

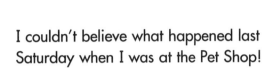

Story Launch

When I was in the pumpkin patch, a funny-shaped pumpkin asked me...

I couldn't believe what happened last Saturday when I was at the Pet Shop!

If I were a farmer, I would grow
_____ (a crop) and have
_____ (animals) because...

When we were camping on the beach, we...

0-7424-1784-0 *After School Writing Activities*

Name _____ Date _____

Story Launch

The magician at my birthday party accidentally turned me into my poodle and my poodle turned into me! So far, my life as a dog…

If I found a treasure buried in my backyard, I would…

When I got home from school, I looked up and saw an alien looking out my bedroom window. He looked like he was trapped, so I…

A Siberian tiger got loose from the zoo today! They said on the news that it was last seen in my neighborhood.

Name _____ Date _____

Story Launch

If I went up in a hot air balloon and floated over my town, I would see...

If I were marooned on an uninhabited island...

If I could read peoples' minds...

While I was working at my computer last night, the screen went blank and the computer talked to me.

Name _____ Date _____

Story Launch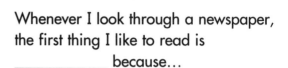

The sport that my friends and I like to watch on television the most is _____ because...

Whenever I look through a newspaper, the first thing I like to read is _____ because...

My _____ (brother/sister/cousin) can be irritating at times, but I appreciate _____ (him/her) most when...

I love to go to the circus because...

0-7424-1784-0 *After School Writing Activities*

Name _____ Date _____

Story Launch

I love celebrating the Fourth of July because…

My favorite season of the year is _____ because…

Reading stories about _____ are the most interesting to me because…

What I like most about where I live is…

Name _____ Date _____

Story Launch

If I could visit any country in the world, I would visit _____ because…

My family is very special because…

It's wonderful being friends with _____ because…

The best part of the last day of vacation was…

0-7424-1784-0 *After School Writing Activities*

Name _____ Date _____

Story Launch

If I were ten years older, I would…

For Halloween, I'd like to go as my hero,
_____, because…

The thing that I love best about
Christmas is…

If I could go on a cruise, I'd like to go to
_____ because…

McGraw-Hill Children's Publishing

107

0-7424-1784-0 *After School Writing Activities*

Name _____ Date _____

Working Out with Words

The ancient Greeks called their poets "word athletes." Today we marvel at the grace and skill of well-known athletes. A good poet shows grace and skill with words.

Reading poetry can be confusing. Some readers wonder, "Why don't poets just say what they mean?" Poets are saying what they mean, but they are also using language that describes how they feel. You can see how Robert Louis Stevenson *shows* in words, not *tells,* in his poem *My Shadow* below.

I have a little shadow that goes in and out with me,
And what can be the use of him is more than I
    can see.
He is very, very like me from the heels up to
    the head;
And I see him jump before me, when I jump into
    my bed.

The funniest thing about him is the way he likes
    to grow—
Not at all like proper children, which is always
    very slow;
For he sometimes shoots up taller like an
    India-rubber ball,
And he sometimes gets so little that there's none
    of him at all.

He hasn't got a notion of how children ought
    to play,
And can only make a fool of me in every sort
    of way.
He stays so close beside me, he's a coward you
    can see;
I'd think shame to stick to nursie as that shadow
    sticks to me!

One morning, very early, before the sun was up,
I rose and found the shining dew on every
    buttercup;
But my lazy little shadow, like an arrant
    sleepy-head,
Had stayed at home behind me and was fast
    asleep in bed.

                    —*Robert Louis Stevenson*

Write a short poem using one of the sentences below.

    The moon shone through the mist.
    The wind blew the snow into large drifts.

Share your favorite poems with a friend and talk about how the poet feels about what he or she is writing about. What kinds of words does the poet use to help you see how he or she feels?

0-7424-1784-0 *After School Writing Activities*

Name _____ Date _____

Working Out with Words (cont.)

A word athlete builds a poem out of different building blocks. A poem often begins with an *image*. An image is a description that makes you feel something. An image helps the reader to see what the poet is talking about. For example, if a writer wanted to tell you that he or she likes to eat pizza, they might say, "I like pizza." You might answer, "Yawn," because "I like pizza" is boring, isn't it? An image that means the same thing might begin:

My nose tingles and my tongue perspires
At the cheese and pepperoni my stomach desires.

See how you don't need to use the word *pizza* if you see the image? But you still know that the poet loves pizza because of the image created with words. Why? Because the poet's nose *tingles* from the smell of a yummy pizza. The poet's *tongue perspires* and *stomach desires*, which mean the poet is hungry for a cheese and pepperoni pizza.

Write another two lines that create an image about pizza. Make the two lines rhyme!

_____

_____

Create an image by writing a poem about your favorite or your least favorite food. For example, you could write about why you like or dislike brussels sprouts. Have a friend write a poem about his or her favorite or least favorite food. Exchange poems and compare words you both used to create your image.

0-7424-1784-0 *After School Writing Activities*

Name _____ Date _____

Poetic Senses

As we have learned, a good rule to follow when writing poetry is *show, don't tell*. Showing not only makes your reader see what it is you're writing about, it also helps them to *smell, feel, taste,* or *hear.* If a poet can make readers use their five senses, it helps them to understand what he or she is trying to say.

Let's go back to the poem on page 109. The *showing* version replaces *like* with *tingles, perspires,* and *desires.* This shows your reader more fully how you feel about pizza. What senses do each of the phrases describe?

1. nose tingles _____
2. tongue perspires _____
3. stomach desires _____

Write a short poem describing what you smell, feel, hear, and taste when you go to your favorite restaurant with your family. Write it so the reader will have the same experience as you do.

_____

_____

_____

_____

_____

Shakespeare is stumped. He wants to write a poem about his favorite place to hang out with his friends. Help him out. Remember to show the five senses by creating images with your words. Read your poems to each other.

0-7424-1784-0 *After School Writing Activities*

Images and Emotions

How does a poet write about how he or she is feeling? Say, for example, you miss your little sister. That's a strong feeling. But writing "I miss my sister" isn't going to tell a reader anything about you or your sister. A good image that would tell a reader that your sister is gone and you have a strong feeling about it, might read something like this:

> There are no sticky fingerprints on my door.

Now your readers want to know why there are no fingerprints on the door. They also want to know if there were ever any fingerprints on the door. You have also used the word *sticky* to give a clue about who might have left a fingerprint. Your could go on:

> The dolls that crowded the stairs are now asleep in her bed.

Now the reader knows that there's a little girl who isn't where you want her to be. The reader has been shown a feeling, or *emotion*, to make them interested in the rest of your poem. Now that you have shown the reader an image that helps them understand how you feel, it is time to give your poem a meaning.

> My little sister Emily will never again snore.
> She's at the hospital, her tonsils to shed.

Try your hand at writing about a powerful emotion you have experienced. You can write about a friend who made you angry or sad, or about a friend or relative that you miss. Put your emotions into a poem.

Ask a friend to help you think of an occasion when you experienced something together that greatly influenced you both. Work together to write a four-line poem that shows the emotion you felt at the time.

Name _____ Date _____

I Wandered Lonely as a Cloud

The poet and critic Ezra Pound wrote that poetry is "news that stays news." He believed that a poem should mean as much today and tomorrow as it did when it was first written. Strong feelings, or *emotions*, remain the same no matter when a poem was written. That is why poets such as William Wordsworth, who died in 1850, are still very popular today. One of his most famous poems begins:

I wandered lonely as a cloud
That floats on high o'er vales and hills,
When all at once I saw a crowd,
A host, of golden daffodils;
Beside the lake, beneath the trees
Fluttering and dancing in the breeze.

Confused? Don't be! What he was writing about and the way he expressed it still portray the way we feel about nature and how it looks today.

1. What is Wordsworth saying in the poem?
   a. That he feels as alone as a cloud in the sky.
   b. That he sees some flowers.
   c. That he has fallen into a lake.

2. What is "fluttering and dancing in the breeze"?
   a. a group of trees
   b. golden daffodils
   c. a lonely cloud

Write your own poem about the beauty of a rainbow or the peaceful feeling you get in nature.

Read other poems by William Wordsworth or James Whitcomb Riley. You and a friend can find them on the Internet or at the library. Even though their poems were written long ago, try to figure out together the meaning or what their poems are describing.

       0-7424-1784-0 *After School Writing Activities*

Name _____ Date _____

Of Cabbages and Kings

A **couplet** is two lines that rhyme.

"The time has come," the Walrus said, "to talk of many things:
Of shoes—and ships—and sealing-wax—of cabbages and kings…."

—Lewis Carroll

A **quatrain** is four rhymed lines of a poem that make a complete thought. A quatrain can be two couplets or four lines in which every other line rhymes. The lines below are marked to show which lines rhyme. The **a** lines rhyme with other **a** lines, and **b** lines rhyme with **b** lines. This is known as a **rhyme scheme**.

Here are two examples of an **aabb** rhyme scheme:

My dog Rusty has lots of bones.   **a**
He keeps them in lots of holes.   **b**
If one is gone, he groans and moans,   **a**
Then goes out on more patrols.   **b**

My mother gets so mad when I don't clean my room,   **a**
She gives me all kinds of strife.   **b**
She opens my door and throws in a broom,   **a**
And threatens to ground me for life!   **b**

Try composing a quatrain with an **abba** rhyme scheme.

Finish the following couplet. Remember to rhyme! Have a friend finish it too and see how many possibilities there are.

The mountain stands majestic and tall

Name _____ Date _____

Five-Line Fun

A **limerick** is a five-line poem with an **aabba** rhyme scheme. Because limericks are usually funny, they are some of the most fun poems to read or write. Writing limericks is also good practice for rhyming and **rhythm**. Rhythm is perhaps the most important poetic device, because rhythm determines the overall sound of a poem.

The rhythm of a limerick is simply achieved by counting the syllables in each line. Lines one, two, and five rhyme and usually contain eight to ten syllables. Lines three and four have a different rhyme and only contain five to seven syllables. An example of a limerick and the number of syllables appears below:

There was an old man with a beard,	**a**	**8 syllables**
Who said, "It is just as I feared!	**a**	**8 syllables**
Two owls and a hen,	**b**	**5 syllables**
Four larks and a wren,	**b**	**5 syllables**
Have all built their nests in my beard!"	**a**	**8 syllables**

—Edward Lear

Now it's your turn to finish a limerick. Make sure you count the syllables and follow the **aabba** rhyme scheme!

_____

who everyone thought was so cool

_____

and talked to a tree

_____

Have a limerick competition. See who can write the most, the funniest, and the cleverest limericks. Don't be afraid to be silly! Have a teacher, friend, or family member be the judge.

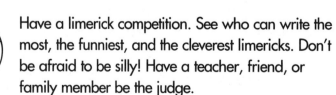

0-7424-1784-0 *After School Writing Activities*

Name _____ Date _____

Japanese Poetic Forms

Haiku and **tanka** are two poetic forms that come from Japan. Both follow a strict number of syllables in each line of the poem. The subjects of haikus and tankas usually have to do with some aspect of nature and contain only a single thought about a special moment.

A **haiku** is a three-line poem of 17 syllables.

Line 1: 5 syllables

Line 2: 7 syllables

Line 3: 5 syllables

The early spring sun	**5 syllables**
Warms the winter-burned meadow.	**7 syllables**
Soon all will be green.	**5 syllables**

The mosquito flew	**5 syllables**
Quickly from its last victim.	**7 syllables**
Next time I'll get her.	**5 syllables**

Write two haikus on the following lines. The first line will start you out.

The fog crept along

_____

_____

_____

My favorite thing

_____

_____

_____

0-7424-1784-0 *After School Writing Activities*

Name _____ Date _____

Japanese Poetic Forms (cont.)

A **tanka** is a five-line poem of 31 syllables.
Line 1: 5 syllables
Line 2: 7 syllables
Line 3: 5 syllables
Line 4: 7 syllables
Line 5: 7 syllables

The mountain lion	**5 syllables**
Sleeps in peace during the day	**7 syllables**
She dreams of her cubs	**5 syllables**
Playfully learning to hunt	**7 syllables**
Now grown to hunt for themselves.	**7 syllables**

Write your own tanka on the following lines. The first line will start you out.

The gold and red leaves _____

_____

_____

_____

_____

To write your own haiku or tanka, go outside and sit for a few minutes. Ask a friend to join you. Notice the sights and sounds around you. Write your thoughts down as a poem. Choose words that will help your reader feel as though he or she had been sitting beside you as you wrote. Exchange your poems and see the differences that you both observed outside.

0-7424-1784-0 *After School Writing Activities*

Name _____ Date _____

As White as the Snow

One poetic device that poets use to paint a picture with words is a **simile**. Remember that a simile usually includes the words *like* or *as* to compare.

In the poem below, Clement Moore used similes to help picture what St. Nicholas looked like. Underline five similes in these lines from *A Visit from Saint Nicholas*.

His eyes, how they twinkled! His dimples, how merry!
His cheeks were like roses, his nose like a cherry!
And the beard on his chin was as white as the snow;
The stump of a pipe he held tight in his teeth,
And the smoke it encircled his head like a wreath;
He had a broad face and a round little belly,
That shook when he laughed like a bowl full of jelly.

—Clement Moore

You're the poet. You want to use a simile that talks about how much you like your new scooter. Which one of the following examples would you use? Circle it.

1. My new scooter is bright red.
2. When I first saw my scooter, I was like a kid looking through a candy store window.
3. I look really cool riding my scooter.
4. I'll never share my scooter with my neighbor Freddie.

Write a short poem using similes to describe how you felt about a present you got for Christmas or your birthday.

Look at the objects in the room where you are sitting. Compare these objects to people you know. Make a list of similes. For example: My grandma is like a comfy chair. Show your similes to your friend and have him or her complete the comparisons.

0-7424-1784-0 *After School Writing Activities*

Name _____ Date _____

You Are a Glittering Star

Using metaphors in poetry helps to create the image that you want your reader to see. A **metaphor** states that one kind of object or idea is something that it really isn't.

Write a metaphor on a separate sheet of paper to express the feelings below. The first two are done for you.

You are happy.
Example: I'm walking on air this morning.

You got an A on a test when you expected to get a C.

The day is hot.
Example: Our house was an oven that day.

You got caught in a rainstorm without an umbrella.

Write a short poem beginning with the following metaphor.

_____ is a glittering star.

_____

_____

_____

Example:
Maria is a glittering star.
It doesn't matter where you are
Her kindness shines through
And she's always true blue.

Write different endings for these two sentences using metaphors. Then write a four-line poem using your metaphors. Have a friend do the same and see what different metaphors you can come up with to express the feeling.

He drank in the beauty of the rainbow.
He drank in…

A ray of sunshine cut the gloom of the fog.
A ray of sunshine cut…

Name _____ Date _____

Poetry Overview

Read the following poem and answer the questions below.

My bedroom windowsill is home to a bird
That never eats worms or flies.
She has a song I've never heard.
She has never flown the skies.

I don't have to buy bird seed.
That's one thing she doesn't need.
My little bird friend will never flee
She's made out of glass, you see.

1. The poem above is an example of
  a. two limericks
  b. two quatrains
  c. two tankas
  d. two haikus

3. What rhyme schemes are used?
  a. abab   aabb
  b. abab   abab
  c. abba   abba
  d. baba   baba

2. The first line is an example of
  a. a tanka
  b. a metaphor
  c. a limerick
  d. a simile

Write one quatrain using one of the rhyme schemes above about a special keepsake or toy that you love.

Write an eight-line poem like the one above with a friend.
Each of you write four lines that rhyme.

0-7424-1784-0 *After School Writing Activities*

What Do Songs Mean?

One of the reasons songs are enjoyed by so many people is because their words, called **lyrics**, mean so much to the listener.

Songs are usually written in verses with a **chorus**, which is repeated throughout the song. Most songs use **end rhyme**, which means the words at the end of the lines of the song rhyme. Like poems and stories, songs have **themes**. This is the message the songwriter is trying to convey to the listener through the song.

Listen to one of your favorite songs while you are looking at the lyrics. Then answer the following questions.

1. What is the song mostly about? _____

2. How does the song make you feel? _____

3. What do you think is the theme of the song? _____

4. How many verses does the song have? _____

5. Does the song use end rhyme? _____ If so, give an example from the song:

_____

_____

6. Does the song have a chorus? _____

7. What is it about this song that makes it one of your favorites?

_____

_____

Use a tune from a song you know and ask a friend to help you write lyrics to go with the music. Be sure to keep your lyrics in the right rhythm with the music. Share your song with friends and family.

Name _____ Date _____

Please Elaborate

Once you've written a first draft, go back and **revise** to make your writing more clear. One way to do this is to **elaborate** by adding details. Using *examples*, *explanations*, and *descriptions* help add more detail.

before revising: Unusual colors glowed in the sky.
after revising: Streaks of green, blue, and red glowed in the sky.

Read each sentence. The hint tells what kind of detail would make the sentence better. Circle the letter of the revised sentence that adds that type of detail.

1. The aurora borealis are beautiful. *(add description)*
   a. The aurora borealis are dazzling, ray-filled curtains of red, blue, and green.
   b. The aurora borealis are a result of charged particles from the sun.
   c. The aurora borealis are often seen in Canada, Alaska, and Greenland.

2. The aurora borealis are made up of glowing particles. *(explain)*
   a. The aurora borealis are bands of red, blue, and green light from the air.
   b. The aurora borealis are a result of charged particles from the sun hitting our air.
   c. The aurora borealis are most often seen in the upper atmosphere.

3. The colors come from different air molecules. *(give examples)*
   a. The colors are dazzling reds, blues, and greens from air molecules.
   b. The different colors come from air molecules such as oxygen, which produces yellow-green.
   c. Nitrogen makes one of the colors of the aurora.

Read each sentence. Then, revise it to add the type of detail given in the hint.
4. The aurora borealis are colorful. *(add description)*

_____

5. The aurora borealis can be seen in the north. *(give examples)*

_____

Write a story about the worst storm you can remember experiencing. Have your friend do the same. Exchange stories and add details to each other's sentences.

Using Commas Correctly

Commas are used to signal pauses or slight distinctions between words in sentences. When you are proofreading your writing, check to make sure that you have used commas properly. They should:

- separate each item in a list of three or more items
- separate two or more adjectives in place of *and*
- set off the words *yes* and *no* or the name of the person you are talking to
- separate the day from the year in a date
- separate the street, city, and state or country in an address

Examples: I had a sandwich, a glass of milk, and a cookie for lunch.

It was a clean, tidy kitchen.

Yes, I'm hungry. Marcus, are you hungry?

She was born on May 23, 1990.

I live at 1046 Mapleview Ave., Bangor, Maine.

Put in commas where they are needed in the following sentences.

1. Camille pushed open the old creaky door.

2. The only things in the room were a desk a chair and a candle.

3. Rudolf are you ready to go? Yes I'm ready to go.

4. They were sent to 47 West 10th St. Abilene Texas to discover the missing clue.

5. The ghost was first seen in the house on December 24 1894.

Make up a story with a friend using the sentences you just added commas to above. After writing it, have your friend proofread it.

Writing Quotations Correctly

Quotation marks show exactly what the speaker said. A conversation in a story is written as a dialogue. When using dialogue, every speaker begins in a new paragraph to make it easier to keep track of different speakers. The first word in a quotation is capitalized. The words within a quotation can end in a comma, question mark, or exclamation point. They never end in a period unless it marks the end of a sentence and are not followed by the identity of the speaker. See the example below.

"Did you go to the Halloween party last night?" asked Kristine.

"Yes, Kristine, I came as a pirate," replied Tuan.

Kristine said, "Who else was there?"

"Just about everyone in our class. It was so much fun. We laughed so hard when Fritz got his head stuck in a pumpkin."

Add the missing punctuation in the quotations below.

1. Where were you at 2:30 on the morning of the fifteenth asked the lawyer.

2. I was in the kitchen replied the witness.

3. And what were you doing in the kitchen he exclaimed.

4. I was making a … a … turkey sandwich he stammered.

5. Exactly what did you put in your turkey sandwich Mr. Boise asked the lawyer, with a triumphant gleam in his eye.

6. The witness licked his lips nervously and whispered Lettuce, tomato, mayonnaise, and bacon.

Write a conversation you've had recently with a friend. Use the correct punctuation marks to show a direct quotation. Ask your friend to do the same. Check each other's quotations.

Name _____ Date _____

Making Subjects and Verbs Agree

Every sentence has a subject and a verb. Present-tense verbs have two forms: the **plain form**, like *walk*, and the **s form**, like *walks*. The verb form must agree with the subject.

When the subject is a singular noun or the pronoun *it, she,* or *he,* use the **s form** of the verb.
Example: Elsa **walks** to school every day.

When the subject is a plural noun, two nouns joined by *and,* or the pronoun *I, you, we,* or *they,* use the **plain form** of the verb.

Example: Elsa and Xenia **walk** to school every day.

Underline the correct form of the present-tense verb in the following sentences.

1. Every day I (jog, jogs) in the park.
2. My brother (run, runs) three miles before school.
3. He (go, goes) around the park four times.
4. My two golden retrievers usually (scurry, scurries) next to me as I jog.
5. Sometimes they (take, takes) off after a squirrel.
6. Two police officers always (pass, passes) us in the park.
7. They (smile, smiles) and (wave, waves) at us.

Write a short diary entry for your favorite TV or book character, telling what you think she or he might be doing now. Use present-tense verb forms. Underline each verb form you use.

Write a story about what you did with a friend last Saturday. Have your friend write a story about the same experience. Trade stories and check to make sure the verb form agrees with the subject. Combine both of your versions of the day into one story.

Name _____ Date _____

Do You Hafe a Brother?

When you proofread your writing or another person's writing, you check to find errors. Check the advertisements below for **spelling errors**, and make sure that the **verb form and subjects agree**. Cross out the misspelled words and write the corrected words above them.

Gum-Everlasting

Does your gum lose its flavor?
Dose it gets hard after only twelve hours?
You need too try new Gum-Everlasting.
WHY?
Yule get all-day chewing enjoyment!

You'll also get our new, high-tech Gum Reflaviator. Put you're old gum inside the Reflaviator befor you go to bed. When you get up in the morning, your gum is sotf, flavorful, and ready for another day. So, bye your Gum-Everlasting today!

Brother Be-Gone

Rose had a big problem—her brothers. When she goed to her room to play with her friends, her brothers allways followed them. Thay teased Rose and laught at her.

Rose tryed Brother Be-Gone. She sprayed Brother Be-Gon around her room. That was the end of her problem! Roses brotters stood by the door, but they could'nt came into her room.

Do you hafe a brother? You need Brother Be-Gone!

Work with a friend to think of two brand-new toys. Each of you write an advertisement for one of the toys. Proofread each other's advertisements for spelling, punctuation, capitalization, and complete sentences.

Proofreading Fun

Symbol	Meaning
∧	Insert a letter, word, phrase, or sentence.
⤶	Take out a letter, word, phrase, or sentence.
⊙	Insert a period.
/	Change a capital letter to a small letter.
≡	Change a small letter to a capital letter.
SP	Check the spelling of a word.

Use these proofreading symbols to help you understand what corrections need to be made in these sentences. Write the sentences correctly on a separate sheet of paper.

1. Everyone knows ∧the best way to keeep fish from Smelling is to cut off their noses.

2. a fence runs all around the the Yard, but never moves ⊙

3. the rug told ∧the floor, "don't move, I've got you covered."

4. The Telephone rang just as I stepped in the door. I quickly answered it⊙What a nice surprise ∧it was to

hear from Uncle joe in Providence, rhode Island. He asked if I would like to fly out ∧to visit him this

summer. I asked my Mom and Dad, and they said I could go. I can't wait. What a thrilling Summer it

will bee!
SP

Write five sentences with two mistakes in each sentence. Have a friend do the same. Trade papers and proofread each other's work.

     0-7424-1784-0 *After School Writing Activities*

Answer Key

Stars Danced in the Sky **9**
1. market bustles; pedestrians swarm; fruit and vegetables crowd; wind breathes; stalls are dressed; scents beckon; street is alive
2. autumn chill threatens; trees wear; leaves are attending a ball; leaves swing, swirl, and waltz; leaves dance; winter sings

Like Distant Drums **10**
1. sky; **2.** tiger; **3.** ice cube; **4.** kangaroo; **5.** sun; **6.** prune

My Brother Was a Prince **11**
1. c; **2.** c; **3.** a; **4.** a or b

Clearly Confused **12**
1. awfully nice; **2.** dim light; **3.** pretty ugly; **4.** once again

Strong as an Ox! **13**
1, 2, 4, 6, 7

Ribbit **14**
1. whirled; **2.** snap; **3.** rattled; **4.** ribbit, chirping, croak, caws, whistles, trills, buzz, racket

Blast! Roar! Crossword **15**
Across
1. wish; **4.** stamp; **7.** slant; **9.** lend; **12.** talked; **14.** raise; **15.** lock; **16.** arouse; **19.** apes; **20.** laid; **21.** aged; **24.** gleamed; **27.** run; **28.** cast; **30.** lies; **32.** totes; **36.** catch; **37.** burst; **38.** err; **39.** pull; **40.** rot; **41.** adore; **42.** alarm; **43.** ensnared; **44.** skim; **45.** use
Down
1. walks; **3.** steal; **5.** toiled; **6.** meet; **7.** stop; **8.** laced; **10.** elude; **11.** dream; **13.** drag; **15.** land; **17.** oil; **18.** froth; **22.** get; **23.** bust; **25.** ate; **26.** pat; **27.** rests; **28.** call; **29.** scares; **30.** lure; **31.** irons; **32.** tear; **33.** order; **34.** trod; **35.** speak; **36.** claim

Comes and Goes **16**
Across
2. less; **5.** moist; **8.** slow; **11.** above; **13.** on; **16.** evening; **17.** laughs; **20.** no; **21.** lent; **22.** guess; **23.** good; **24.** stop; **25.** her; **26.** he; **27.** many; **28.** son; **31.** men; **33.** out; **35.** right; **39.** obey; **41.** own; **43.** doer; **44.** swim; **45.** die; **46.** mild; **47.** wet; **48.** straight
Down
1. ma; **2.** loved; **3.** even; **4.** sent; **5.** mighty; **6.** ill; **7.** tough; **9.** lass; **10.** won; **12.** below; **14.** none; **15.** bigger; **18.** guest; **19.** hero; **24.** snub; **26.** hot; **29.** now; **30.** them; **31.** my; **32.** new; **34.** under; **36.** idle; **37.** go; **38.** trim; **39.** old; **40.** east; **42.** went; **44.** sea

Thesaurus **17**
1. decent; **2.** sizable; **3.** beneficial; **4.** pleasant; **5.** undamaged

Animal Expressions **20**
1. k; **2.** f; **3.** p; **4.** b; **5.** i; **6.** d; **7.** m; **8.** a; **9.** n; **10.** e; **11.** c; **12.** j; **13.** l; **14.** g; **15.** o; **16.** h; **17.** q

The New World **21**
Transition words used may vary.
First, he studied maps and thought he could sail west to Asia. Second, he asked the king of Portugal for ships, but the king refused to help Columbus. Next, he asked for a royal commission from Spain for ships, but they would not help him. Then, in 1492, King Ferdinand and Queen Isabella, rulers of two Spanish kingdoms, gave him the ships he needed for the voyage. Finally, Columbus set sail for Asia, but he discovered the Americas instead.

The Tipsy Tugboat Tooted Its Horn **22**
1. alliteration—Six swans swam by.
2. alliteration—The tipsy tugboat tooted its horn as it tossed in the waves.
3. alliteration—Mr. Reilly really wanted to ride on a roller coaster.
assonance—Reilly ride
4. assonance—Helene sighed when I replied that we couldn't look for shells in the rising tide.
5. consonance—Two taxi drivers tackled the thief.

All the King's Horses **23**
1. Benjamin Franklin said, "Early to bed and early to rise, makes a man healthy, wealthy, and wise."
2. "I am always doing that which I can not do in order that I may learn to do it," Pablo Picasso stated.
3. "All sorrows can be borne if you put them into a story or tell a story about them," Isak Dinesen, the Danish author wrote.

4. "All for one and one for all," wrote Alexandre Dumas, the French dramatist. It was the Musketeers' motto in The Three Musketeers.

Writer's Toolbox Crossword **25**
Across
2. hyperbole; **7.** metaphor; **9.** point of view; **11.** foreshadowing; **12.** alliteration
Down
1. consonance; **3.** assonance; **4.** onomatopoeia; **5.** simile; **6.** personification; **8.** hook; **10.** tone

The New Kid **26**
Story Map
1. a. setting: beginning of fourth grade, Hillcrest Elementary School
 b. characters: Mr. Brunswick, the class, and me
 c. problem: My family moved to Seattle this summer. I'm the new kid here.
2. first event: First, Mr. Brunswick introduced me to the other kids in the class.
3. second event: Next, some of the kids teased me about my southern accent.
4. third event: Then, one courageous girl said she'd show me around the school.
5. resolution: Finally, other kids welcomed me to Seattle and Hillcrest Elementary School.

Bigfoot **27**
I. A. Appearance: Bigfoot has brownish fur, looks like half-man, half-ape, and is up to or over seven feet tall. Bigfoot walks erect on thick legs.
 B. Where is it found? Bigfoot lives in wilderness areas of North America, especially the Pacific northwest.
II. A. Evidence
 1. In 1967, a Bigfoot was caught on film by Roger Patterson in northwest California.
 2. Human-shaped tracks were discovered from 12 inches to 17 inches long.
 3. There have been several expeditions and sightings.
 4. Cultural histories of Native Americans include many stories and beliefs of a hairy, man-like creature.
 B. Explanations
 1. The man-like creature may simply be a large bear.
 2. When bear tracks in snow melt, they may look like huge footprints.

First... Next... Then... . . . . **28**
First: Mix two parts water with one part flour.
Next: Stir until the mixture is smooth, sticky, and wet.
Then: Blow up a round balloon and tie the end.
Fourth: Dip strips of newspaper into the mixture.
Fifth: Apply the strips to the balloon.
Sixth: When the newspaper is dry, cut out a hole in the bottom, burst the balloon, and paint it orange.
Finally: Cut out a face for the pumpkin.

Walfredo and the Cat **29**
1. a, f, g, i; **2.** a

Grabs Your Interest **34**
1. For 4,300 years, the Great Pyramid of Khufu at Giza was the tallest building in the entire world. **2.** b; **3.** c

Tornado Warning! **35**
1. a, c, f; **2.** c, d, f; **3.** a, d, f

And She Lived Happily Ever After **36**
1. c; **2.** a; **3.** b

The Title Is Vital **37**
1. c; **2.** Titles will vary but should give a clue to the story without giving away the ending.

Hoot! **38**
1. Boy, was she surprised when the play ended.
2. At the time, he thought it was nothing to worry about.
3. No one expected what happened in the park after school. Sentences will vary.

Mrs. O'Leary's Cow **39**
1. a; People in cities chose school boards too.
2. b; Fires cause a lot of damage all around the world.

Wrapping It Up **40**
1. b; **2.** a

Welcome to the Show! **41**
1. taste, smell; **2.** sound, sight; **3.** sound, sight, touch; **4.** sight; **5.** touch, sight; **6.** sight; **7.** smell; **8.** sight, sound. Descriptions will vary.

0-7424-1784-0 After School Writing Activities

Answer Key

Mystery at the Museum 42
1. c; **2.** b; **3.** b

Missing Ring 43

Cause	Effect
1. when they were left out in the open	The ring, piece of quartz, and key were stolen
2. When Mrs. Rockwell, Muriel, and Mr. Malinski discovered their items were missing	Mr. Malinski called Detective Cage to ask for his help
3. Detective Cage wanted to solve the crime	so he looked for clues
4. he found an important clue	Detective Cage found out who took the missing ring

Solving the Case 44
1. when; **2.** how; **3.** where; **4.** how

Showing How You Feel 45
1. b; **2.** d; **3.** f; **4.** c; **5.** e; **6.** a; **7.** d

Putting It All Together 46
Across 6. end; **7.** point of view; **10.** hook; **11.** climax; **12.** plot;
13. beginning; **14.** characters
Down 1. transitions; **2.** middle; **3.** title; **4.** resolution; **5.** conflict; **8.** setting;
9. dialogue

True Stories (Nonfiction)

Why I Should Keep Morgan 52
1. a; **2.** c; **3.** c

Volcano Erupts! 53
1. b; **2.** c

Extra! Extra! 57
1. Who: Thaddeus Briggs
What: saw an unidentified flying object, round object surrounded by a very bright white light
When: 9 P.M., March 29
Where: corn field at Lone Pine Farm in Sioux City, 50 feet off the ground, then sped north
2. It was really a <u>peculiar</u> sight. I <u>wasn't exactly frightened—just startled</u>," Briggs stated.

Today I... 62
<u>Facts</u>
On the way to school, I found a dollar.
I took it to the school office.
The secretary told me that if nobody claimed it, I could have it at 3 o'clock.
Finally, 3 o'clock arrived.
The secretary smiled and handed me the bill saying, "Nobody claimed it."
On the way home, I bought two comics.
<u>Opinions</u>
Today was pretty lucky.
I think it must have fallen out of somebody's pocket.
I felt nervous when I went into the office.
I felt great.

Realistic Fiction 75
I thought she was a government spy.
When I got on the bus, she greeted me in at least 12 different languages!
She got out and picked up the bus and moved it over.
A sports car driven by an evil-looking man started chasing the bus. Our bus outran the evil man.
When I got to school, television reporters were there. They wanted to talk to our bus driver. They said she was a film actress who was learning how to be a bus driver for a movie she was making. She didn't talk to any of the reporters, though. She went inside a trailer and refused to come out.
I thought about Lakeesha and how much she looked like the substitute bus driver movie actress. They were the same person!

Science Fiction 76
air pollution; water shortage; water pollution; food shortage; land pollution

All the World's a Stage 78
1. tragedy; **2.** comedy; **3.** comedy

Red Badge of Courage 82
1. the setting; **2.** the Civil War; **3.** a soldier; **4.** Answers will vary.

Punch Line 88–89
B. a pun

3. He showed her something that, to her, looked like a figurine of a ladybug and said, "This is what I have for collateral."
2. The loan officer's name was Ms. Patty Whack. When the frog told Ms. Whack that he wanted a loan, she asked if he had collateral.
6. The bank president said, "Why, that's a knick knack, Patty Whack. Give that frog a loan."
5. She asked, "Do you know what this is, and should I give him the loan?"
4. She took it to the bank president and said, "There's a frog out there who wants a loan, and this is what he has for collateral (showing him the figurine)."
1. A frog went to get a loan at a bank.

Myths 92
Answers will vary.

The Moral of the Story 94
1. c; **2.** answers will vary

Poetic Senses 111
1. feel and smell; **2.** and taste; **3.** feel and taste

I Wandered Lonely as a Cloud 112
1. a; **2.** b

As White as the Snow 117
5 similes—cheeks were like roses, nose like a cherry, the beard on his chin was as white as the snow, smoke it encircled his head like a wreath, shook when he laughed like a bowl full of jelly
2. When I first saw my scooter, I was like a kid looking through a candy store window.

Poetry Overview 119
1. b; **2.** b; **3.** a

Proofreading

Please Elaborate 121
1. a; **2.** b; **3.** b
Sentences 4 and 5 will vary but should match the hints given.

Using Commas Correctly 122
1. Camille pushed open the old, creaky door.
2. The only things in the room were a desk, a chair, and a candle.
3. Rudolf, are you ready to go? Yes, I'm ready to go.
4. They were sent to 47 West 10th St., Abilene, Texas to discover the missing clue.
5. The ghost was first seen in the house on December 24, 1894.

Writing Quotations 123
1. "Where were you at 2:30 on the morning of the fifteenth?" asked the lawyer.
2. "I was in the kitchen," replied the witness.
3. "And what were you doing in the kitchen?" he exclaimed.
4. "I was making a ... a ... turkey sandwich," he stammered.
5. "Exactly what did you put in your turkey sandwich, Mr. Boise?" asked the lawyer, with a triumphant gleam in his eye.
6. The witness licked his lips nervously and whispered, "Lettuce, tomato, mayonnaise, and bacon."

Making Subjects and Verbs Agree 124
1. jog; **2.** runs; **3.** goes; **4.** scurry; **5.** take; **6.** pass; **7.** smile, wave

Do You Hafe a Brother? 125
Gum-Everlasting

Dose—Does	you're—your
gets—get	befor—before
too—to	soft—soft
Yule—You'll	bye—buy

Brother Be-Gone

goed—went	Roses—Rose's
allways—always	brotters—brothers
Thay—They	coouldn't—couldn't
laught—laughed	came—come
tryed—tried	hafe—have
Be-Gon—Be-Gone	

Proofreading Fun 126
1. Everyone knows the best way to keep fish from smelling is to cut off their noses.
2. A fence runs all around the yard, but never moves.
3. The rug told the floor, "Don't move, I've got you covered."
4. The telephone rang just as I stepped in the door. I quickly answered it. What a nice surprise it was to hear from Uncle Joe in Providence, Rhode Island. He asked if I would like to fly out to visit him this summer. I asked my Mom and Dad, and they said I could go. I can't wait. What a thrilling summer it will be!